PILGRIMAGE

PILGRIMAGE

Meditations on a Journey of Faith

PATRICIA D. BROWN

Abingdon Press
Nashville

PILGRIMAGE
MEDITATIONS ON A JOURNEY OF FAITH

Copyright © 2007 by Patricia D. Brown

This book is printed on acid-free paper.

Library of Congress Cataloging-in-Publication Data

Brown, Patricia D., 1953-
Pilgrimage : meditations on a journey of faith / Patricia D. Brown.
p. cm.
Includes bibliographical references.
ISBN 978-0-687-64464-3 (binding: pbk., adhesive perfect : alk. paper)
1. Christian pilgrims and pilgrimages—Prayers and devotions. 2. Christian life. I. Title. \

BX2323.B76 2007
263'.041—dc22

2007001117

07 08 09 10 11 12 13 14 15 16—10 9 8 7 6 5 4 3 2 1
MANUFACTURED IN THE UNITED STATES OF AMERICA

To view life as a pilgrimage is, in part,
a description of life as the result of living it.
The journey is life itself.
It is a journey of faith.

CONTENTS

INTRODUCTION

This book is intended to give you the opportunity to take some quiet time apart and reflect on your unique spiritual journey—your "journey of faith." Your journey is much like a pilgrimage experience, for every pilgrimage begins with a call from God. A pilgrimage is a personal invitation to go deeper into the fullness of Christ. The word *pilgrim* comes from the Latin *peregrinus*, which means "stranger," denoting a person who travels to a foreign place. In a sense, we all are pilgrims wandering here on earth, trying to find our true faith. It is a journey back to the heart of God.

Two paths converge in the making of a pilgrimage: the actual and the spiritual—a specific destination and a perpetual journey. In other words, your spiritual pilgrimage is not detached from your physical pilgrimage on this earth. Both require you to leave "home." Both require discomfort and sleeping away from your familiar "bed."

I made my first literal pilgrimage several years ago in the "great fifty days" between Easter and Pentecost when I took a group to France. We longed to travel to where the people of the Middle Ages had walked great distances under arduous conditions on pilgrimages inspired by faith. My understanding of pilgrimage took shape in my mind gradually on this trip—and even now continues to form. Although my pilgrimage was undertaken with a group, it was a very personal and singular act of devotion. I wanted to receive the blessing that pilgrimage would bring. I saw the pilgrimage as an opportunity to do something motivated by my faith, and for no other reason. Each person in our group had his or her own motivation, and each derived a particular result or benefit from it. Likewise, you will have your own reasons for pilgrimage, and you will reap your own unique benefits from the experience.

A Brief History of Pilgrimage

Jesus was the pilgrim par excellence. His initial venture was from the heart of God into the heart of our human reality. Since Jesus' time, sacred sites have been the objects of pilgrimage. In the middle of the third century, the early Christian Origen wrote about his trip to the Middle East: "There is shown at Bethlehem the cave where He was born.... And this site is greatly talked of in surrounding places."[1]

In the fifth century, monks from Egypt made pilgrimages to Jerusalem. Many decided to stay in the region, planting themselves in the Judean wilderness outside the city. This developed into a regional center for Christian monasticism. Pilgrimage was also a striking phenomenon in the Middle Ages. Throughout the eleventh and twelfth centuries, great European pilgrimage centers were established when Christians were deprived of access to the Holy Land by Muslim occupation.

The church in Rome tried unsuccessfully to control the pilgrimage routes, offering indulgences and forgiveness for certain journeys. But people took willingly to the road, imposing penances on themselves. Soon an entire industry grew up along pilgrimage routes. The abbeys gave lodging and organized pilgrimages from one place to another, and a number of organizations and hospices provided aid and protection.

The act of pilgrimage continues today, telling us that it must have enduring worth. In its dramatic simplicity, it invites us to root ourselves imaginatively in the past even as we search for the spiritual center of our being.

A Pilgrimage of Your Own Design

Make plans now for a pilgrimage of your own design. If you are able to travel abroad, you might visit the medieval pilgrimage routes in Great Britain, France, Italy, or Spain—or the Holy Land sites of Bethlehem and Jerusalem. If you plan to travel in the United States, you might consider visiting the monastery home of Thomas Merton in Kentucky or the Mission

Churches of the Southwest. Or, if you prefer to stay close to home, your pilgrimage might include a local religious retreat center or a church in your own neighborhood. Take time to lay flowers at the grave of a loved one. Simply designate a time—thirty minutes, an hour, or more—and make a pilgrimage. Walk your neighborhood and notice the flowers, trees, sand, and rocks. Walk in gratitude. Pray for the homes and families you pass. Recall that God is present in the ordinary places of your life, too.

Whatever you plan, take this little book of meditations with you to illuminate your path. Use the margins as a journal to record your thoughts and prayers in order to glean the most from your pilgrimage experience.

Planning a Pilgrimage Abroad

If you plan to take a pilgrimage abroad, get out a map of your chosen country and plot your course. You may choose to join with a group of pilgrims, such as my fellow-travelers did. This simplifies the nuts and bolts of such detailed travel. If you plan to travel alone or with a companion, begin by making your travel arrangements. Contact the monastery and convent guest houses where you plan to stay; buy your plane ticket; and secure your train pass or bus tickets or rent a car that will help transport you to the holy sites. Before you board your plane, break in your new walking shoes and pack a light bag.

Two weeks before your departure date, begin with thoughtfulness and prayer to meditate on the thirteen daily readings of part 1. These will serve as inspiration points as you enter into the deeper preparation for pilgrimage. If you are inspired and find it helpful, you may want to string a set of prayer beads, secure a walking stick, or read other books on historical and modern-day pilgrimages.

As the day of your departure nears, invite some friends or family to join you in "A Prayer for Pilgrimage" (see p. 17). This is a special blessing that uses the symbols of water, to remember your baptism; prayer beads, a cross, and a shell, to represent your prayers; and oil, to use in anointing as a healing presence on the journey. It is always in order on such an occasion to read from the Gospels and, if a celebrant is present, to celebrate the Eucharist.

How to Use This Book

Whether you are a pilgrim traveling abroad or a stay-at-home pilgrim seeking to deepen your devotional life, you will find the reflections in this book useful for a daily time of personal examination and journaling. Because it is a forty-day journey, you may choose to use the book during the season of Lent, a traditional forty-day observance of repentance and self-reflection. If you like, gather some friends together and make a study out of it (see *Meeting with a Group*, p. 14, for details). There are many people who want to expand their spiritual lives. You'll discover lots of common threads as you share and compare the all-too-common aspects of life lived while on the "pilgrimage route."

An Overview of the Journey

The book is divided into three parts. *Part One: Preparing for Pilgrimage* is about spiritual preparations for life. As I share the preparations I made for my first literal pilgrimage, which included the preliminaries of packing my bags to preparing my soul, you, too, will feel challenged to pack—or unpack—some of your own emotional and spiritual baggage that keeps you from being on "The Way" with Christ.

Part Two: Pilgrim on the Way focuses on what it means to be a "pilgrim on the Way." As I share my deepest reflections from such pilgrimage sites as Mont Marie in Paris and the tidal island of Mont St. Michel, you will find yourself reflecting on the sites of your own life—the homes in which you've lived and the places that have claimed you at certain times in your life.

Part Three: Home Is the Journey delves into the ups and downs of what it means to return to your everyday, ordinary, post-pilgrimage life as a different person. Of course, it will be a journey of the heart for most of you. But even as you rise to live another seemingly ordinary day, you will have a renewed sense that you are part of something bigger. You are part of an extraordinary "pilgrimage" adventure—a journey to a deeper awareness of your relationship with God.

Each Day's Journey

Make each reading a part of your day's journey whether you are at home or traversing the French countryside. Each reading is laid out in a manner that is easy to follow.

Introduction

A Psalm

First there is a psalm from the Hebrew Scriptures. This short, inspirational text offers you the space and time to quiet and center yourself before taking your first step. Whether you are reading the book alone or with others on a literal pilgrimage, remember to pause for a few minutes of silence and reflection before continuing. Even a few minutes in quiet meditation can calm your mind and open your heart, bringing you more deeply into the moment. Then, from that place, you will be able to more effectively assimilate the day's reflection and gradually surrender yourself to God, your guide.

Pilgrimage Reflection

Next comes the day's Pilgrimage Reflection. Each day I share personal stories and things I have observed and learned about God, myself, and others. I wrote these readings for people who want to join me on a journey of discovery, looking for ways to mature and move into a practice-centered life of prayer. I have drawn on the wealth of faith-based practices from Christian tradition—across centuries and communities—to write in ways that speak to each of us wherever we are in our journey of faith. In keeping with Wesley's "catholic spirit," I embrace the gifts that Christians of past ages have conferred to us. They hold a vast storehouse of experience from which we can extract ways of traveling with God. As you explore these routes with me, I hope you will find the integrity that will help you be humble and honest in your spiritual life. My further hope is that by encouraging the exploration of pilgrimage as a form of prayer, and by expanding the arena through the examination of practices used in different cultures throughout the two thousand years of Christian history, you will discover new ways to encounter the Divine that will deepen your spirit in both your faith and in your understanding of God.

These Pilgrimage Reflections are designed to help you think about your own spiritual growth and development. It is helpful to use these readings for reflection (ask: *What does this reading say to me?*) in combination with a brief period of meditation (ask: *Where and how is God saying this to me?*). Whether alone or traveling on pilgrimage with others, pause and reflect on personal life experiences that come to mind. If you are with others, share with one another. When we tell our stories in the context of our faith, we become aware of how God is present to us. And when we consider our lives carefully, with our hearts as well as our heads, God touches us in greater ways than we ever imagined.

Introduction

Moments of Devotion

The next segment, Moments of Devotion, offers wishes and hopes that we want to incorporate into our lives. These "May I" moments will help you think further about the issues of your own life. They can easily be turned into prayers that will draw you closer to God. If others are with you, take turns sharing. Let each person answer the question, "Where does this moment touch my life?"

Some Things to Think About

Each day's reading ends with Some Things to Think About. These questions will help you to "debrief" and travel further. If in a group, reflecting on your own experiences and putting them into words will help you come to thoughtful conclusions about your spiritual journey and discover any next steps you may want to take. Sharing and discussing these experiences with others will help you clarify your feelings and sort through your intuitions to live in spirit-filled ways. Remember to keep the focus on the workings of the Holy Spirit to help you grow in faithfulness.

Meeting with a Group

If you choose to make a study of the book, your group might choose to meet weekly (for six weeks), reading the previous week's daily entries before the meeting. As you gather together, take time to greet and catch up with one another.

At your first meeting, you might want to use the prayer ritual found on page 17 to initiate yourselves into the pilgrimage process. In future meetings, plan to use an opening ritual such as praying together or lighting a candle or sharing food.

Next, take the time for each participant sojourner to share his or her favorite passage and some personal reflection from the seven days of reading assigned for the week. Then go around a second time to discuss Some Things to Think About, like those found on page 15. It is not necessary to cover all the suggested questions—only those that pertain to you or your group. Share as time allows.

Finally, as you prepare to close your time together, share a closing ritual or prayer. This may be praying together the Lord's Prayer, also known as the Our Father, or holding hands while each shares a short benediction.

If you prefer to meet every two weeks, plan to have three festive evenings of good friends, food, and conversation around the three parts of the book. I did this myself and enjoyed cooking and serving a full meal of French cuisine with salmon and crème fraîche, baguette, apple tart, and wine from the Bordeaux region.

The Journey Begins Now

If you are reading this pilgrimage book as a personal devotional guide, try to be open to what your own prayerful encounters, along with common sense, have to teach you. Throughout the book I share practices and methods that have changed my life since I began to create an inner room for God. These writings contain some of the understandings that have come to light as I have struggled to put God into my journey of the "everyday." I pray that they also will help you as you seek a more vital relationship with God.

Remember that whether you travel near or far, in pilgrimage you will find a place where you belong—not a place on a map, but a place in your heart. You will discover the place where life really is as it should be. You know this deep in your bones and in your heart of hearts. After all, the journey of faith is a journey of the heart. May your journey make you more attentive to the needs of the world around you and create a sacred space in which you move past your differences with others to find commonality and community.

Some Things to Think About

- If you were to take a pilgrimage to a far-off place, where would you like to go and why? Would you go with someone, or would you go alone? Why?
- A pilgrimage, great or small, is a microcosm, a picture of your life. What do you think your trip might reveal?
- Where are your present places of pilgrimage, the places where you go to remember and meet your heart? What have you learned in these places?

A PRAYER
FOR PILGRIMAGE

Merciful God, your glory fills the universe, and I find your presence wherever I go. Be with me now on my pilgrimage, surround me with loving care, protect me from every danger, and bring me safely to my journey's end. **Amen.**

Put some water on your head or shoulders.
I receive this water and remember my baptism. I am a pilgrim who is thankful. **Amen.**

Place a cross or prayer beads around your neck.
I receive this rosary/cross as the sign of Christ's cross upon me. I am a pilgrim who prays. **Amen.**

Place a touch of oil upon your forehead or on the backs of your hands.
I receive this oil and am anointed. I am a pilgrim who is a healer and reconciler. **Amen.**

O Lord, my God, to you and to your service I dedicate this pilgrimage.
I devote myself, body, soul, and spirit.
Fill my days with the record of your wonderful works;
　　enlighten my understanding with the light of your Holy Spirit, and
　　my heart and will to center in what you have planned for me.
In prayer, quicken my devotion;
in praises, heighten my love;
and through your Word, extend your clarity.

(Adapted from *Book of Common Prayer* [New York: Oxford University Press, 1990], pp. 562-63.)

PART ONE:
PREPARING FOR PILGRIMAGE

O Lord, all my longing is known to you;
my sighing is not hidden from you.
My heart throbs, my strength fails me;
as for the light of my eyes—it also has gone from me.
My friends and companions stand aloof from my affliction,
and my neighbors stand far off.
Those who seek my life lay their snares;
those who seek to hurt me speak of ruin,
and meditate treachery all day long.
But I am like the deaf, I do not hear;
like the mute, who cannot speak.
Truly, I am like one who does not hear,
and in whose mouth is no retort.
But it is for you, O LORD, that I wait;
it is you, O LORD my God, who will answer. (Psalm 38:9-15)

❧ Day 1: Sometimes I Feel a Rumbling

I am at a place of waiting as I stand on my back porch watching the last of the sun go down. In my stream of life, a voice comes to my ear: "Make a pilgrimage. Go to ancient sites. Go somewhere with other seekers. Go anyway you can. Just go!" I have been restless lately, feeling a bit lost. Yet I sense that there is a deeper voice hidden in my soul. Sometimes I feel it rumbling just below the surface. At times it recedes—and I go on about my life buying the groceries, picking up the shoes, watching another sitcom—but it never leaves. In moments of panic—"Why am I doing this? What am I looking for? What do I seek?"—it is in full voice.

Now I have made my plans and I am going on pilgrimage. Why? Is it because I yearn for memorable experiences or holy events and places that I can remember and imbue with sanctity? Am I looking for opportunities to renew my dedication and stimulate my devotion? Or perhaps it is to find a sense of healing, holiness, and peace.

Seeking the Heavenly Jerusalem

In the fifth century, monks from Egypt went on pilgrimage to Jerusalem. Many stayed, planting themselves in the Judean wilderness outside the city and making the region a center of Christian monasticism. These early ascetics saw themselves, not as part of the earthly Jerusalem, but as part of the heavenly one: "But the other woman corresponds to the Jerusalem above; she is free, and she is our mother" (Galatians 4:26). They went to wait in the hope of the heavenly Jerusalem, the city that was to come.

The archetype of pilgrimage continues today, telling me that it must have enduring worth. In its dramatic simplicity it invites me to root myself imaginatively in the past even as I search for the spiritual center of my being—that inner core where the Holy Spirit is at home with my spirit and we live as one.

The ancient church knew the distance it was inviting people to travel. As the days between Jesus' ascension and his return grew, it felt at times as if the chasm between the seeker and the incarnate God was simply too great. Therefore the seeker was taught to navigate the distance one step, one day, one season, one question at a time. *What do I seek? How do my longings and my life story connect with God's story? Am I willing to reorder my life so that I can hear and follow Christ?* These threshold questions, asked of inquirers entering into the ancient rite of Christian initiation, echo back to us. Through Advent waiting and Christmas light, through Lenten fasting and Easter vigil, and on into Pentecost, candidates reflected upon their life story in the light of the gospel story.

What do I seek, since I leave all that I know to find it? I seek an inheritance "imperishable, undefiled, and unfading, kept in heaven" for me (1 Peter 1:4-6). Why do I seek this? I seek this so that I can make it through the hard times of testing to once again walk in the light. "Rejoice, even if now for a little while you have had to suffer various trials, so that the genuineness of your faith—being more precious than gold that, though perishable, is tested by fire—may be found to result in praise and glory and honor when Jesus Christ is revealed" (1 Peter 1:6-7). Jesus said to his followers, "I go to prepare a place for you" (John 14:2). I call this habitation heaven, the heavenly Jerusalem.

As Columbanus, sixth-century Celtic monastic founder, expresses so beautifully, "Let us concern ourselves with things divine, and as pilgrims ever sigh for and desire our homeland; for the end of the road is ever the object of travellers' hopes and desires, and thus, since we are travellers and pilgrims in the world, let us ever ponder on the end of the road, that is of our life, for the end of our roadway is our home."[2]

Moments of Devotion

May I reorder my life so that I can hear and follow Christ.

Some Things to Think About

Three threshold questions, asked of inquirers who enter into the ancient rite of Christian initiation, are now yours to consider:

- What do you seek? What is happening in your life that prompts your search?
- How do your longings and life story connect with God's story? What place does faith have in your life?
- Are you willing to reorder your life so that you can hear and follow Christ? Are you willing to do this by making a disciplined exploration of Christian living and service to God and neighbor? What might this mean for you?

Come, O children, listen to me;
I will teach you the fear of the LORD.
Which of you desires life,
and covets many days to enjoy good?
Keep your tongue from evil,
and your lips from speaking deceit.
Depart from evil, and do good;
seek peace, and pursue it. (Psalm 34:11-14)

❧ Day 2: Elsewhere Is the Kingdom of God

How strange that I would leave home to find myself. This is not the first time.

When I was twelve, I left home to go to church camp. I had earned fifty cents an hour babysitting and had tucked twenty-two dollars, a fortune, into my panty drawer bit by bit each Friday night of the long Pennsylvania winter. For that one week I wanted to live perfectly: to love everyone, to pray on my knees in my cabin, to guard every word and gesture. My reward came my third year with the admiring applause and coveted trophy inscribed "Best Girl Camper." The title gave me a free week the following year.

Now, I again leave home to camp in a distant place. I go in order to be somewhere else, to be someone else. I extricate myself from my bad habits and routines to go elsewhere, to an extraordinary place, where I can be the "other" whom I long to be. I move to a place beyond the mundane reality of my daily experience. I am a woman who often lives in harsh judgment of myself wanting to find perfection. Am I again in search of that most perfect expression of myself?

I purposely choose to "de-center" myself, to live for days off-kilter in order to enter a kind of existential psychodrama. Somehow I know, intrinsically, that this moving away from myself is essential, for without it I cannot rediscover the girl within. I experience again what I've always known about spiritual formation: it is only when I reach for a center other than myself that I am able to move forward and recover myself. So I go, wanting to be touched by the outward-growing power of the pilgrimage. I cry, "Elsewhere! Elsewhere is the Kingdom of God, peace!"[3]

Moments of Devotion

May I risk moving away from myself to experience and rediscover the child within.

Some Things to Think About

- When have you "left home" to find yourself? What did you discover about yourself? What did you find out about God?
- What bad habits and routines do you want to extricate yourself from in order to be healthy and whole? How do these habits and patterns of living hurt your spirit: body, mind, and relationships?
- What new ways of being and doing might you adopt that can help you to live in healthier, more wholistic ways?

Let the words of my mouth and the meditation of my heart be acceptable to you,
O LORD, *my rock and my redeemer. (Psalm 19:14)*

🌑 Day 3: Beads and Baubles

One day I was on my way home from a speaking engagement. A billboard announced a bead store at the next exit. I pulled off the highway and into a shopping-center parking lot. The woman in the store sold me fifteen strings of ten purple, diamond-cut beads along with string and wire. I felt pleased with my purchases. Only when I got home did I realize that I had no idea where to begin to make my prayer beads, known in these later centuries as a rosary.

How did this string of beads we call the rosary get its name? Thomas of Contimpre of the Western church seems to be the first, around 1250, to call this a rosary—*rosarium maning*, or rose garden. Perhaps he felt that we most truly enter into the spirit of the prayer beads when we enter it as a rose garden. We contemplate the thorns and the red blood, but we find peace in the joy of the garden. The moments we spend with a rosary are moments spent in a garden of love. I too wanted to experiment and experience time with my Creator in this garden of love.

That's when Cynthia, my neighborhood "bead lady," adopted me along with my project. We sat in her cozy workroom under an intense light. I was enthralled with the complex process as she began to open little drawers and packages. Beads of all shapes and sizes began to accumulate in front of me. Then she magically added purple silk thread, tiny seed beads to place between the larger beads, along with a silver cross and scallop shell for the "tail." Finally, Cynthia chose a few larger glass beads to serve as mystery beads: the joyful, the sorrowful, the glorious, and the luminous. I was delighted.

It took me a couple of hours to string the collection together in the correct fashion. Cynthia did the more detailed work with the use of pliers and her magnified eyeglasses. In the end, the result was worth the effort. They were magnificent, the most beautiful beads I'd ever seen—if I do say so myself.

Praying with Beads

Praying with beads has been a beautiful and inspiring Christian prayer practice since the early centuries of the church. Numbered beads were made of cord, pebbles, or seeds and worn as necklaces or wrapped around the waist, wrist, or fingers. They were used to count prayers and mantras (repeated phrases or sayings) and even to aid memorization of the 150 psalms. Some make a string of ten beads and pray the Ten Commandments or name ten things for which they are thankful. Others use them to pray for ten different people or needs, one for each bead.

During the Middle Ages, prayer beads became common in every part of Christian Europe. Olive wood, taken from the trees of the garden of Gethsemane and carved into beads, was (and still is) a special prize. Christians in the tenth century used a string of knots, either tied into a circle or in a straight strand, to pray the Lord's Prayer and other repetitive prayers. These beads were often carried in a pocket or tied around one's wrist or neck for easy access. People, taking seriously the mandate to pray always, wore a prayer cord around their waists so that the beads were in easy reach whenever a hand was free.

Most rosaries hold only five decades—five sets of ten beads—and to do the complete rosary, a person travels around the strand four times.

I want it all, which is why my rosary has all twenty decades. Nothing less seems quite right.

Moments of Devotion

In my meditations and prayers, may I not settle for less than what seems good and right.

Some Things to Think About

- What objects do you have that have religious significance? Where did you acquire them? What spiritual meanings do they hold?
- How might you create a set of prayer beads for yourself? What would they look like? How would you use them? What colors would you use? What would be their texture?
- Prayer beads can contain any number of beads and can be used in an unfolding number of ways. If you were to make yourself a simple string of seven beads, what would you pray? The fruit of the Spirit—love, joy, peace, patience, kindness, gentleness, and self-control?

Good and upright is the LORD;
  therefore he instructs sinners in the way.
He leads the humble in what is right,
  and teaches the humble his way.
All the paths of the LORD are steadfast love and faithfulness,
  for those who keep his covenant and his decrees.
For your name's sake, O LORD,
  pardon my guilt, for it is great. (Psalm 25:8-11)

❧ Day 4: Unfinished Business

The invitation to pilgrimage is an invitation to repent. Repentance is a godly sorrow, so deep as to cause one to change. "Repent, and believe in the good news" (Mark 1:15). "Unless you repent, you will all perish as they did" (Luke 13:3). Repent or perish.

The Cavalier Santo Brasca, a servant at the court of the duke of Milan in the late fifteenth century who pilgrimaged to Jerusalem, said, "The pilgrim should prepare himself to pardon the injuries done to him; to restore everything belonging to others; and live according to the law, because without this first and necessary disposition every hope and every fatigue is in vain."[4]

" 'He that be a pilgrim,' declared the London preacher Richard Alkerton in 1406, 'oweth first to pay his debts, afterwards to set his house in governance, and afterwards to array himself and take leave of his neighbours, and so go forth.' "[5]

My credit card bill is paid to date. My school loan is outstanding. Jeannine, a friend, will care for kid and kittens. Orin, next door, will keep watch of our house. With my life set in order, the time arrives to be a pilgrim, to go forth.

As I prepare my heart for this journey, I have a strong need to set matters right with those with whom I may have unfinished business. It is a wish to set out with a clear heart, with absolution of my past sins. It is a serious review of my life. I feel that in taking stock I will be better prepared to receive significant movements of the Spirit within. Can it be that preparation for pilgrimage is preparation for a new kind of life?

Moments of Devotion

May I let go of any anger and revenge I still hold for the injustices done to me.

Some Things to Think About

- When did someone hurt you? How did they make amends? How did you feel afterward?
- How did your family of origin deal with hurt feelings? How do you make things right with someone you have wronged?
- What matters need to be set right within your own household?
- Stop procrastinating and take stock now. Make a list of three matters that you will clear up in the next two weeks. Remember, preparation for pilgrimage is preparation for a new kind of life.

O LORD, God of my salvation,
    when, at night, I cry out in your presence,
let my prayer come before you;
    incline your ear to my cry.
For my soul is full of troubles,
    and my life draws near to Sheol.
I am counted among those who go down to the Pit;
    I am like those who have no help. (Psalm 88:1-4)

❧ Day 5: Early Martyred Saints

The year my husband, Richard, died, I packed up with our four-year-old son and headed south to Quito, Ecuador. I went where no one called me "that poor widow." Being thought divorced was freedom of a kind.

Each year, when the crocuses push up through the spring snow, I travel to Richard's grave. Common sense tells me he is not there. Spirit-sense tells me he is. It is the one place I continue to go when I need to remember earlier times when my whole life still stretched out before me and possibilities were numerous. We "talk," and I am reminded of my mortality. I reflect on my pilgrimage from the cradle to the grave. He "whispers" to me to remember our son, our love, our Savior; those things that are eternal. Pretensions, ambitions, and schemes come to an end at this place, the grave. It is as if God stoops down with Richard and shares that moment of my most ordinary life; together they say to me, "Bone of [our] bones and flesh of [our] flesh" (Genesis 2:23), and they ask me to live quietly, according to God's will, until through death Christ's mission is complete in me.

In the first three centuries of the church, the bodies of the martyred saints were revered. People would gather at their burial sites on the anniversaries of their deaths to keep their memory alive. They celebrated the Lord's Supper followed by an agape feast—a special time of food and fellowship.

I'm not so different with Richard's memory. He is my early martyred saint, and his grave is my holy place of pilgrimage.

Moments of Devotion

May I be present in this moment and grateful for all the people in my life, recognizing that all but love is impermanent.

Some Things to Think About

- Do you have an "early martyred saint"? If so, who is it, and where is your "holy place of pilgrimage"?
- What event in your life caused you to set aside your pretensions, ambitions, and schemes? How did your life change because of the event?
- Recognizing that all but love is impermanent, name ten people whom you are grateful for in your life.

Truly God is good to the upright,
   to those who are pure in heart.
But as for me, my feet had almost stumbled;
   my steps had nearly slipped.
For I was envious of the arrogant;
   I saw the prosperity of the wicked.
For they have no pain;
   their bodies are sound and sleek.
They are not in trouble as others are;
   they are not plagued like other people.
. . . .
When my soul was embittered,
   when I was pricked in heart,
I was stupid and ignorant;
   I was like a brute beast toward you.
Nevertheless I am continually with you;
   you hold my right hand.
You guide me with your counsel,
   and afterward you will receive me with honor.
                        (Psalm 73:1-5, 21-24)

❧ Day 6: Pilgrim Par Excellence

Jesus was the pilgrim par excellence. His initial venture was from the heart of God into the heart of our human reality. At the age of twelve, he and his mom and dad went as pilgrims to Jerusalem for the Passover. There he found himself drawn to the temple (Luke 2:41-52).

Jesus lived the life of a wanderer. He was born in a barn, and his parents soon fled to Egypt to save his life. Jesus' ministry was one of homelessness. He called his disciples to sit with children, to tell stories on the hillsides, and to touch the people in the streets. God's self-emptying in the incarnate Christ was God's act of self-exile. He chose to travel with us. He took upon himself a pilgrimage of the heart. This profound phrase, uttered at the end of his journey, sums it up: "I came from the Father and have come into the world; again, I am leaving the world and am going to the Father" (John 16:28).

Jesus said to his disciples, "Wherever you enter a house, stay there until you leave the place. If any place will not welcome you and they refuse to hear you, as you leave, shake off the dust that is on your feet as a testimony against them" (Mark 6:10-11). The story goes on: "So they went out and proclaimed that all should repent. They cast out many demons, and anointed with oil many who were sick and cured them" (Mark 6:12-13).

Jesus called together his main followers and began to send them out two by two. He gave them instructions to "take nothing for their journey except a staff; no bread, no bag, no money in their belts; but to wear sandals and not to put on two tunics" (Mark 6:8-9).

The Early Pilgrim's Outfit

Pilgrims during the Middle Ages had special outfits for the journey. Dressed as penitent travelers—broad-brimmed hats shielding their heads and wallets or pouches swaying across their backs—they carried a long, iron-shod cane called a pilgrim's staff.

I've packed too much! My little suitcase is overflowing. So I throw it all upon my bed and begin again. My staff will make my way easier. I take no food, for I don't need the added temptation. In fact, I hope to fast on occasion. I take only one bag—more than enough for carrying up staircases without assistance. I take some money, but only for necessities. My souvenirs will be my memories and a few pictures that I expect to receive from others. Sneakers substitute for my usual summer sandals, and I carry on the plane a brand spanking new red parka that will keep me warm and dry—and be easy to pick out in a crowd. This is important because I am to be the director of this group of vagabonds.

Moments of Devotion

May I mindfully acknowledge the impermanence of "stuff," letting go of all greed, and desire only experiences that lead me further along my spiritual path.

Some Things to Think About

- Make a list of belongings that you have to wash, dust, sweep, and repair. Consider if you truly need them.
- What can you give away in order to simplify your life? Make a list of ten items along with how you will dispose of them.
- Have you ever packed for a trip only to discover that you can't get your suitcase closed? What did you remove?

Our steps are made firm by the LORD,
  when he delights in our way;
though we stumble, we shall not fall headlong,
  for the LORD *holds us by the hand. (Psalm 37:23-24)*

❦ Day 7: A Rattle and Ring

I like the idea of having a walking staff hooked like a crosier, like the early pilgrim leaders.[6] It seems official. Maybe I'll go all out and have my crosier finished on the top, as some did, with a hollow ball that doubles as a musical instrument. I will rattle it at appropriate times. I might, if only for a moment, feel as Miriam did when she rattled her tambourine, leading God's people to the promised land.

Lately I've had an urge to quit—to lay down my staff, to withdraw, to walk no more. Yet something in my "deep" calls me to be always "on the way"—the way that leads to love and self-giving, the way that leads to God. Helen Bacovcin, noted translator of the Eastern classic "The Way of the Pilgrim," reflects, "The Pilgrim is deeply in love with his God and never tires of communicating with Him.... He knows as few of us do that a wholehearted response to the message of the Gospel is the only one that makes sense and satisfies the very core of our being."[7]

Sometimes I feel as if I am in a fog and can't see three feet ahead. But I've learned to keep on. It doesn't matter that I am feeling uncertain or confused or afraid. All of these feelings disappear when I place myself fully in the arms of Jesus, who promised to see me through the dark places.

I'll pack a walking stick, minus the embellishments. Yet, a musical instrument of some sort might be helpful, so I'll pack a soothing C-tone. The small, gold bell slides lightly into my pocket. In my mind's ear I hear its gracious call to fellow pilgrims in a bus terminal or cathedral, tenderly calling us to community. If the bell doesn't work, I'll still have the stick!

Moments of Devotion

May I face the painful experiences that are an inevitable part of life with compassion for myself and othrs, instead of repeating the stories of injury that increase my suffering.

Some Things to Think About

- Recall the times when you have wanted to lay down your staff of leadership and quit. What did you do instead?
- When and where have you found the hope to travel on when your journey got rough? What advice would you give to others?
- Remember a time when you extended compassion to a fellow traveler. What were the circumstances? What did you do to aid the person?

My steps have held fast to your paths;
*   my feet have not slipped.*
I call upon you, for you will answer me, O God;
*   incline your ear to me, hear my words. (Psalm 17:5-6)*

❧ Day 8: A Leery Pilgrim

It is not easy to be a pilgrim. To be a pilgrim is to be a disciple, even when my own interests are at stake. There are dangers and uncertainties. The journey involves hardships and excitement. When I was young, I was eager to face any risk. Now that I'm older, I'm more often cautious than excited. I don't want to be hurt on the road or ill-treated at home. I am not sure what kind of pilgrim I am, and I'm a bit leery that I may find out.

Pilgrimage is more than religious tourism. The act of pilgrimage itself embraces The Way while walking with the One who is the Way. It is a living, moving, breathing metaphor for the disciplined Christian life. Pilgrimage without an interior journey is just a trip.

Some who accompany me on this pilgrimage will have little concept of what this interior journey is, and they will meet themselves en route in surprising, and at times disturbing, ways. They, like me, will meet the shadow side of their being in the process of the journey. And just as I must do, they must say, "Isn't it interesting what this experience is doing inside of me?" If we are truly awake, we will be able to confront our sin and embrace God's forgiveness. Isn't this calming embrace of God the unstated hope of each one of us?

At such times as these, when I feel disappointed in my own actions and reactions, I recall the words of the apostle Paul: "I pray that, according to the riches of his glory, he may grant that you may be strengthened in your inner being with power through his Spirit, and that Christ may dwell in your hearts through faith, as you are being rooted and grounded in love. I pray that you may have the power to comprehend, with all the saints, what is the breadth and length and height and depth, and to know the love of Christ that surpasses knowledge, so that you may be filled with all the fullness of God" (Ephesians 3:16-19).

Moments of Devotion

May I lovingly remember that others, like myself, are still growing spiritually, and may I forgive their offenses as I forgive my own so that I can live as one who has a heart of compassion.

Some Things to Think About

- What "pushes your buttons"? Recall the last time someone or some situation "pushed your buttons." Were you "awake" enough not to

41

blame the other person but to take responsibility within yourself? Why or why not?

- What are some of the things that can prevent you from asking yourself "Isn't it interesting what this experience is doing inside of me?" What does this question help you discover?

- In what ways are you strengthened in your inner being with power through God's Spirit so that Christ dwells in your heart through faith? How has this helped you be rooted and grounded in love?

I will give thanks to the LORD *with my whole heart;*
I will tell of all your wonderful deeds.
I will be glad and exult in you;
I will sing praise to your name, O Most High. (Psalm 9:1-2)

❧ Day 9: Because I Am

For many, a pilgrimage is an exaltation, a time to give thanks. I like to think that this voyage is primarily a way of visiting, adoring, and contemplating the holy mysteries of God. The early pilgrims were not merely going to a place; they were going to a place to meet a person. Likewise, the goal of my journey is God—God's self, not an "experience," but the one and only reality.

Douglas Vest, Episcopal priest and spiritual director, writes this in his book on pilgrimage:

> G. K. Chesterton sagely noted that what the world needs are not more wonders but more wonder. Victor and Edith Turner, after years of studying the anthropology of pilgrimage, commented that if mysticism is interiorized pilgrimage, pilgrimage is exteriorized mysticism. My brief rendering of these sentiments is that a guiding theology needs to accompany me on pilgrimage. A helpful beginning is to allow childlike wonder in my encounters, to invite God on my trips as well as on life's "journey," and to trust that God's story and mine intersect in both everyday and extraordinary ways.[8]

With childlike wonder I am reminded that all of my life belongs to God. Apart from God, my life has no meaning, no hope, no way. I exist only because of "I Am." We give God claim of our whole beings, and gently but inexorably, God, who is perfect Love, asks from us total response: all we have and are in every sphere and activity of our lives.

Moments of Devotion

Because my past, present, and future all belong to God and I am made in the image of God, may I live in ways that honor our love relationship.

Some Things to Think About

• How have you experienced "childlike wonder" recently?
• Where was God in the midst of these "everyday and extraordinary ways"?

I call upon you, O LORD*; come quickly to me;*
give ear to my voice when I call to you.
Let my prayer be counted as incense before you,
and the lifting up of my hands as an evening sacrifice.
Set a guard over my mouth, O LORD*;*
keep watch over the door of my lips.
Do not turn my heart to any evil,
to busy myself with wicked deeds
in company with those who work iniquity;
do not let me eat of their delicacies. (Psalm 141:1-4)

❧ Day 10: Break in an Ordinary Life

Pilgrimage was a striking phenomenon in the Middle Ages. It involved men and women, singles and married with families, young and old, all classes and every category of life. Most who traveled saw it as a break in an otherwise ordinary life. The Celtic monastic tradition produced an above-average number of wanderers. Many traveled to the Holy Land and other famous shrines of Christendom. For other pilgrims of this era, the pilgrimage created the perfect context to steal away from their village—all in the name of God. However, there were some who took to pilgrimage as a lifestyle.[9]

I ask the same questions that Brother John of the Taizé community in France did about the pilgrimage phenomenon. He asked, "Does it imply a turning away from earthly commitments, an escape to the dream world of the past? These questions prompt us to look at the Bible in an attempt to deepen our reflection on the *meaning* such a practice assumes in the light of faith. Are we beholding a passing fashion, or is something more essential involved here?"[10]

I will go and find out for myself.

Moments of Devotion

May I recognize paths that divert me from my true goals and travel only the roads that offer me wisdom, insight, and spiritual growth.

Some Things to Think About

- How can we discern the difference between times when we have faithfully followed God versus incidences when we have simply indulged "passing fashions" of the religious times?
- Recall one or two of the stories from the Bible that demonstrate risky behavior. How can you emulate these actions in your own life?
- Be brave and experiment in your relationship with God by being in relationship with others in new ways. Take risks. Or, as Martin Luther said, tongue in cheek, "Sin boldly!"
- Do you dream of breaking out of your ordinary life in order to get a fresh perspective? How might you do this?

Whom have I in heaven but you?
  And there is nothing on earth that I desire other than you.
My flesh and my heart may fail,
  but God is the strength of my heart and my portion forever.
Indeed, those who are far from you will perish;
  you put an end to those who are false to you.
But for me it is good to be near God;
  I have made the Lord GOD my refuge,
  to tell of all your works. (Psalm 73:25-28)

❧ Day 11: I and Thou

The truly wise know that God lives within one's self; there is no need to travel thousands of miles to meet God. So, why do I leave home, leave the familiar? Because I often miss seeing the eternal. Not because it is not present in the miniscule, but because it simply cannot be recognized without the experience of the panoramic. I cannot see the "I" within until I have experienced the "Thou" without.

It gives me pause to read the pilgrim's report of a wise elder's words to a critical parishioner: "Believe that your hatred is caused by the fact that you are not firmly grounded in the love of God and you are not interiorly secure and at peace with yourself."[11] Franciscan Brother Ramon says it with a bit more grace, although with the same bluntness: "While the faithful people of every tradition go on their pilgrimages with devotion and intense fervour, the saintly ones know that unless God is to be found within their own experience, such pilgrimage is useless."[12] Amen!

A great amount of preparation has been poured lovingly into this journey, but the end will be determined by God. It is clear that whatever the details of preparation for this journey, the task that is uppermost in my mind and heart is the more delicate task of spiritual preparation. My mind turns to the "inner space" that must be created so that the Spirit can do the formation work within.

Moments of Devotion

May I remember that unless God is to be found within my own experiences, my pilgrimage is lacking.

Some Things to Think About

- Where have you found God in your own experiences?
- How can you begin to create new "inner space" so that the Spirit can work within you?
- As you review your life, when have you missed seeing the eternal? How did you miss God in those moments?

May God be gracious to us and bless us
and make his face to shine upon us, Selah
that your way may be known upon earth,
your saving power among all nations.
Let the peoples praise you, O God;
let all the peoples praise you.
Let the nations be glad and sing for joy,
for you judge the peoples with equity
and guide the nations upon earth. Selah
Let the peoples praise you, O God;
let all the peoples praise you.
The earth has yielded its increase;
God, our God, has blessed us.
May God continue to bless us;
let all the ends of the earth revere him. (Psalm 67:1-7)

❧ Day 12: I Want a Blessing; I Need a Savior

I want a blessing for my journey. In the Middle Ages, those seeking to claim the privileges and blessings of an authentic pilgrim obtained a written authorization from their bishop or abbot. An ordinance of King Richard II of England in 1388 indicated that any pilgrim without such *testmoniales* risked arrest. Otherwise, the devout might be mistaken for an adventurer or profiteer.[13]

So, I turn in my mind to the ways I might secure a written script of blessing and permission—some symbol of my sincerity. My Methodist bishop might puzzle over the request. Would he understand? I can ask. At worst, he can only say no.

In the meantime, this tenth-century Celtic blessing and prayer will suffice.

> May this journey be easy, may it be a journey of profit in my hands!
> Holy Christ against demons, against weapons, against killings!
> May Jesus and the Father, may the Holy Spirit sanctify us!
> May the mysterious God be not hidden in darkness,
>   may the bright King save us!
> May the cross of Christ's body and Mary guard us on the road!
> May it not be unlucky for us, may it be successful and easy! [14]

> Now I pray to Thee, God the Father eternal, through this pilgrimage of Thy dear Son, that He may watch over us on this our pilgrimage through this vale of tears, and safeguard us from the satanic enemies of our souls, and cast down the idols, that is the domination of sin in our hearts, that we may meet with Christ Our Lord through this pilgrimage, and be called back to the Promised Land, Amen.[15]

Moments of Devotion

May I remember all my days that it is the Lord who blesses me and keeps me; the Lord who makes his face to shine upon me, and who is gracious to me; the Lord who lifts up his countenance upon me, and who gives me peace. *(Based on Numbers 6:24-26)*

Some Things to Think About

- When have you sensed an authentic feeling of peace with God? Where were you? What were the circumstances?

51

- Who has blessed you on your journey? Parents? Teachers? Pastors? Friends? The poor?
- Whom have you blessed on your journey? Children? Parents? Colleagues? The homeless?
- Life does not always have to be hard. In fact, at times it is easy and comfortable. The sun shines and we get the "A." What blessings have you experienced in the past day, month, or year? List them.

"This is my resting place forever;
here I will reside, for I have desired it.
I will abundantly bless its provisions;
I will satisfy its poor with bread.
Its priests I will clothe with salvation,
and its faithful will shout for joy.
There I will cause a horn to sprout up for David;
I have prepared a lamp for my anointed one.
His enemies I will clothe with disgrace,
but on him, his crown will gleam." (Psalm 132:14-18)

◐ Day 13: Passageway

I need some symbol to mark my journey—perhaps a gleaming crown like the one given to the psalmist. Or perhaps some rite of passage should send me off from this place to that. A special order of ceremony seems called for. In medieval times, this took the form of blessing the pilgrim's pouch and mantle and presenting the pilgrim with a staff from the altar. This ritual presentation of the pilgrim's staff bore a striking resemblance to the dubbing of a courageous knight or to the ordination of a priest.

Other, more austere pilgrims put on traveling clothes resembling a monastic habit as a way of marking themselves for the journey. The habit was a long, brown, coarse, homespun gown with large sleeves. Embellishments could include patches made in the shape of a cross, a leather belt around the shoulder or loins, and a large, round hat decorated with scallop shells or small lead images of Mary and the saints.

It was not uncommon for a pilgrim to wear a rosary of large beads hung around the neck or arm with a bowl, bag, and a scrip (a wallet to keep travel documents secure) suspended from it.

I find myself smiling. How pleasantly funny to picture myself in such an outfit. Of course, I won't dress so. I'll be sensible. But I want to be just a touch outlandish lest I appear too staid. So I attach three small scallop shells from the Florida seashore to a silken cross and place it on the lapel of my coat.

> Give me my scallop-shell of quiet,
>   My staff of faith to walk upon;
> My scrip of joy, immortal diet;
>   My bottle of salvation;
> My gown of glory, hope's true gauge,
> And thus I'll take my pilgrimage![16]

Moments of Devotion

May I clearly see and enjoy the whimsical moments of life and relish their light touch upon my steps.

Some Things to Think About

* Recall the rites of passage that have been important in your life. What events have they marked? A wedding to celebrate a marriage? A

baptism to mark new life in Christ? A funeral or memorial service to attend to the death of a friend?

- How have these rites of passage shaped the person you are today?
- Take stock of the mementos and keepsakes that you surround yourself with to remind you of your journey. What are the stories behind them? Share your story of one of these items.

PART TWO:
PILGRIM ON THE WAY

O LORD, *you will hear the desire of the meek;*
  you will strengthen their heart, you will incline your ear
to do justice for the orphan and the oppressed. (Psalm 10:17-18a)

❧ Day 14: A Labyrinth of Emotions

The moment of our arrival produces a torrent of emotion within me—mostly relief that we have safely traversed the corridors, elevators, escalators, and revolving doors without loss of bags or people. We've arrived, although spirits lag somewhat behind.

Destinations are not all that they may seem. The destination is more transient than it first appears. It is indeed an end point, yet it is also the beginning of a new portion of my adventure; and I am reminded that I will always be a stranger on this earth. The journey simply is.

There is a part of me that would like to arrive somewhere. I want a fixed point. Having one would suit my need for certainty. But I arrive and discover that the destination so longingly anticipated is not the real destination; it is only one more rest stop along the way. As soon as I land at a door or gate, a whole new vista opens up and another mystery begins. Still, reaching some marker along the way, I search for an appropriate ritual to distinguish each place and day. I reflect on my original hopes. I've sought many things. One or two have been found, including a labyrinth.

In the Middle Ages people took "on the spot" pilgrimages by creating labyrinths. Marked out on the floor of the Chartres Cathedral, the labyrinth served as a substitute for the pilgrimage to the Holy Land. The holy place, symbolized in the design, takes on the equivalent of an adventurous journey full of perils. The essential of a pilgrimage is evident: motion toward a center.

As I begin the twisted walk laid out before me on the floor, other members of the group are walking too. As I step carefully, I review their hopes, which I've begun to listen to, one by one. Each pilgrim on this journey is at a different place on the discipleship journey, just as each is at a different place on this labyrinth. Not further ahead or lagging behind, not higher or lower, not faster or slower, just different.

Moments of Devotion

May I possess the humility to assess my strengths and my weaknesses so that I may recognize my interrelatedness to my companions on the journey.

Some Things to Think About

- Destinations are not all they may seem. The destination is more transient than it first appears. What destination are you nearing that will open you to begin a new adventure?
- Birthdays are usually celebrated with cake and candles. What other rituals serve as markers along your way?

O come, let us sing to the LORD;
   let us make a joyful noise to the rock of our salvation!
Let us come into his presence with thanksgiving;
   let us make a joyful noise to him with songs of praise!
For the LORD is a great God,
   and a great King above all gods.
In his hand are the depths of the earth;
   the heights of the mountains are his also.
The sea is his, for he made it,
   and the dry land, which his hands have formed.
O come, let us worship and bow down,
   let us kneel before the LORD, our Maker! (Psalm 95:1-6)

❧ Day 15: Worship

How wonderful to worship God here at Mont Marie—in a place and a way that brings me closer and closer to God and to others. And as I worship, God's self is the giver to me of all that God is—Love. All this becomes even more wonderful as I draw nearer to the wonder of God in praise and adoration.

I get the feeling that some travelers in our group may have expected worship "experiences" or happy sensations. Some yawn as if bored—or fail to show altogether. Is God more fully worshiped if I feel pleasure or satisfaction? Who is at the center of my worship? The worshipers or the One worshiped? Is the worship I offer worthy of God? It does seem, in this modern Protestant movement, that the primary concern is for the reaction of the worshiper. Are these pilgrims too accustomed to everything being organized to appeal to the congregation, to provide an experience, to make them comfortable or involved?

Worship is not entertainment. Any time worship gets skewed in such a way that there is a performer and an audience, something is terribly, terribly wrong. God is always the audience. We are the worshipers playing out the salvation drama in God's presence.

Here in this wondrous basilica it is my responsibility to adjust to the mystery of the worship—not the other way around. Hearing the Mass in French must be reminiscent of the people of the Middle Ages hearing Mass in Latin. I find the worship to be worthy: fine, beautiful, shapely, orderly, and graceful. It makes intuitive sense, even if it does not provide an emotionally satisfying experience at all times. There is mystery and awe. I am privileged to catch a bit of God's conversation and a glimpse of God's awesomeness through the eyes of the local worshipers—through how they view God and express their understandings in worship.

Moments of Devotion

May I open my eyes to see the mystery all around me so that I may enjoy the ephemeral rainbows of every moment.

Some Things to Think About

- Recall moments during community worship when you experienced the mystery of God. Share one exceptional moment.
- Who is the audience in the worship services you attend? Why do you think so?

For it was you who formed my inward parts;
  you knit me together in my mother's womb.
I praise you, for I am fearfully and wonderfully made.
  Wonderful are your works;
that I know very well.
  My frame was not hidden from you,
when I was being made in secret,
  intricately woven in the depths of the earth.
Your eyes beheld my unformed substance.
In your book were written
  all the days that were formed for me,
  when none of them as yet existed. (Psalm 139:13-16)

❧ Day 16: The Mystery of Paix

Each day I participate with this small band of pilgrims in the Eucharist. As we participate together, we participate with others in the sacrifice and self-offering of Christ. In our bonding, we are presenting his healing presence to the world once again. Mystically, theologically, and intuitively I know that in the Eucharistic action of the Body of Christ, as in no other way, we take part in the act of sacrificial obedience to the will of God.

This morning we gather at a side altar to make Eucharist. We lay out the fair linen and place the chalice, wine, and bread upon it. Together we repeat the ancient words—these words that have been knit into our hearts.

The Lord be with you.

And also with you.

We are, in a real sense, reconstituting the Body of Christ—weaving back together the bits and fragments of that body and assembling it into wholeness once again.

Lift up your hearts.

We lift them up to the Lord.

We are participating in the mystical re-presentation of the Incarnation itself.

Let us give thanks to the Lord our God.

It is right to give God thanks and praise.

We are becoming made into the likeness of Christ. And we are doing this together in a way that none of us could accomplish alone.

Holy, Holy, Holy, Lord God of hosts. Heaven and Earth are full of your glory. Hosanna in the highest. Blessed is the One who comes in the name of the Lord. Hosanna in the highest.

We are, in a sense, raising up the true Body—the Body of Christ—once again into the world.

The Eucharist continues to unfold discretely, piece by piece. We raise our voices to give the responses.

Through your Son Jesus Christ, with the Holy Spirit in your holy church, all honor and glory is yours, almighty [God], now and for ever.

It is the mystery of the Spirit that fills the air and gives our adoration perfect expression.

Together we say the Lord's Prayer, and we exchange the kiss of peace—"Shalom," "Peace," and in French, "Paix." We lift the cup. We remember that we are one communion and that we can be whole again. We break bread. We remember the passion story about the mending of broken hearts. As Alan Jones writes, "The Church is the place where the wonderful story that will make us into one People is told over and over again. It is a Love Story about the mending of broken bones; it is a Passion Story about the joy of homecoming."[17]

I wonder why this love story continues to knit itself to us. Whatever the reason, I accept it.

Moments of Devotion

May I hold the mystery of the Spirit that fills the air and gives my adoration perfect expression.

Some Things to Think About

- These Eucharistic words from the third century continue to be used today to celebrate the feast of bread and wine. What is their meaning to you?
- The word *Eucharist* means "great thanksgiving." For what do you give God thanks?

But I, through the abundance of your steadfast love,
  will enter your house,
I will bow down toward your holy temple
  in awe of you.
Lead me, O LORD, *in your righteousness. (Psalm 5:7-8a)*

❧ Day 17: The Cathedral

I stand in the twenty-first century in front of this thirteenth-century cathedral window depicting Joan of Arc. I watch people come and go. Some come to Orleans as tourists, others as pilgrims. The tranquility of the cathedral presents a strong contrast to the world outside. It is timeless. This place suits a dual function. One is material, and the other is symbolic. This cathedral offers a communal expression of the love of God.

Our tour host is "reading" the cathedral to us using her technical, historical, and religious knowledge. There is no one level on which the cathedral can be read and appreciated. No single meaning is valid. Each person understands the cathedral in relationship to his or her intellectual and spiritual journey. An enlightened symbol of transcendent faith, a prayer, an architectural and technical wonder, a place of renewal or penance—the cathedral is all of these things and more.

I am enthralled by the stained glass of this sanctuary. In one panel, Saint Joan sits in full armor upon her horse. In a second, the flames lick at her knees as her eyes gaze upward. I imagine the awe that the scenes must have struck in the hearts of medieval pilgrims.

I stand in the middle of the aisle, at once small and great. The glass, the spires, and the cross all speak to me of eternal truths. Yes, I see the skills of generations in the majestic structure. The cathedral stands before me as a vast witness to the God of the universe. In this complex and mysterious monument I reflect on the meaning of life and reconsider my place. This cathedral, like many others, is under repair. But that is the way of cathedrals; they are living things, always undergoing renewal.

> And I saw the holy city, the new Jerusalem, coming down out of heaven from God, prepared as a bride adorned for her husband. And I heard a loud voice from the throne saying,
> "See, the home of God is among mortals.
> He will dwell with them as their God;
> they will be his peoples,
> and God himself will be with them."
> (Revelation 21:2-3)

I look around to see where others of our entourage have gone. It seems difficult to keep the attention of our modern tour group for more than a few minutes. We are an anxious lot and have a short attention span. Is it that our senses are deadened with the myriad of images to which we are exposed? I wonder if, at times, there is just too much to see and experience in so short a time. I think so. Our souls need time to catch up with our feet.

We leave Orleans, God's home among mortals. God is making all things new. A new Jerusalem. A new community. Timeless.

Moments of Devotion

May I slow my pace enough on the road to allow my soul to catch up with my feet.

Some Things to Think About

- Where do you find expressions of God's love?
- Our lives are much like cathedrals—living things, always undergoing renewal. How is your life experiencing renewal?

I live as an alien in the land;
  do not hide your commandments from me.
My soul is consumed with longing
  for your ordinances at all times. (Psalm 119:19-20)

❦ Day 18: Hospitality

I am humbled and amazed at the generous hospitality we receive from the Benedictines here at Mont Marie. Although these sisters are set apart for their work of adoration and praise, they are not insular. I am grateful that they hold a high standard of hospitality. I've climbed the mountain of stairs to this summit to rest and find healing from the bumps and bruises of this day, and in this place I am extended hospice and care.

Hospitality for the Ages

In the Middle Ages, at the height of the pilgrimage industry, monasteries provided hospitality and charity to poor pilgrims who could not afford inns. Hospitals, ecclesiastical property, and priestly households also were routinely used by travelers.

It isn't that the accommodations here in this house are lavish or the food haute cuisine. Instead, these modern-day saints give me their presence. The French word *attendre* means "to wait." They attend to me in their listening, eye contact, and invitation to evening Vespers. That is what they do. They wait. They give me time to climb the stairs, find the dining hall, and turn to the proper page for prayer.

At evening prayer, to my relief, one of the sisters dressed in the white garb speaks English. She hands me the prayer book with pages thirteen and forty-nine marked. She asks why I am on pilgrimage. I tell her, somewhat haltingly, that I am hoping for a blessing.

The organ peals. We take our respective places for the worship to come, she in the choir and I in the nave. Another sister leads the congregation in song. A priest walks up and down the long aisles sprinkling water on expectant heads. I, like the worshipers around me, bow and make the sign of the cross on my head and chest—in the name of the Father, the Son, and the Holy Spirit.

I am encouraged as we set off for Vézelay the next morning. I leave the basilica happy and at peace, filled and floating with hospitality. These Benedictines call me to an attitude of hospitality among my fellow travelers. Hospitality involves exchange. There is a giver and a receiver. I remember that the give-and-take of good conversation is as much about thoughtfully receiving the observations of others as it is about sharing my own. One of Saint Benedict's clearest mandates was that of hospitality: "Receive all guests as Christ."[18] I look and see the face of the Divine in them.

Do they see Christ's face in me?

I, the recipient, am called upon to receive humbly and with gratitude, knowing that each gift is from the hand of God. I cannot begin to calculate or speak of the worth of all that I am giving and receiving. All I know is that the gift is extravagant.

Moments of Devotion

May I walk humbly and with gratitude, knowing that each gift I receive is from the hand of God. And God's gift is extravagant.

Some Things to Think About

- Where have you seen the face of Christ? How did you know that you were experiencing the Divine?
- When have you been extended hospice? How were you cared for, and when did you extend care?

Make me to know your ways, O LORD;
teach me your paths.
Lead me in your truth, and teach me,
for you are the God of my salvation;
for you I wait all day long.
Be mindful of your mercy, O LORD, and of your steadfast love,
for they have been from of old.
Do not remember the sins of my youth or my transgressions;
according to your steadfast love remember me,
for your goodness' sake, O LORD! (Psalm 25:4-7)

❧ Day 19: Uncommon Prayer

Today we travel to Taizé to pray with Brother Roger and the community. Called common prayer, the liturgy of the hours, or the daily office, the Latin word is *officium*, a word that means "duty." If these acts of worship and praise are a responsibility, they are not burdensome. The brothers here structure their daily lives around times of prayer and praise.

For most of our pilgrimage group, this is new. Our usual practice is to pray "on the fly," without organization or pattern. An undisciplined lot, we squeeze in an occasional devotional. Prayers are at our convenience, made up along the way according to our mood of the moment. We pay no mind to the Christian calendar or readings of the week. We are led by our whims. Except for Sunday mornings, we pray in isolation, disconnected from other believers, and thereby finding ourselves increasingly disconnected from God.

The Daily Office

The tradition of daily office, called by many names through the years, is a time when certain prayers are prayed at fixed hours of the day or night. The two most common times of prayer are morning and evening, traditionally called Lauds (Morning Prayer) and Vespers (Evening Prayer). In this prayer practice, the psalms are read, scripture lessons are heard, prayers are offered, and silence is kept.

Their beauty is in their simplicity, for once the ins and outs of the practice are learned, worshipers begin to notice the powerful sequence of readings, the mood of the psalms, and the presence of God more readily—not just in that moment but throughout their day. This brief, intimate daily conversation with God is a way of saying, "Good evening" and "Good morning—I'm just checking in."

I carry a new, red, traditional prayer book, the pocket-sized edition. Our small band of seekers structures its days of pilgrimage around the ancient tradition of common prayer, morning and evening. When possible, like today at Taizé, we join another community in its praise. Other times, our small troop prays the daily litanies during the in-betweens of the road. We are Protestant protesters rediscovering the daily office.

This place called Taizé, like the daily office, is off the beaten track. Our professional driver has never before been here. It is not on the map. Yet

Taizé welcomes more than 100,000 pilgrims from sixty countries each year. How can this gift of community remain virtually unknown—except to those who are seeking?

In Memory of Brother Roger

In August 2005, 2,500 people were gathered together for worship at the ecumenical Christian community called Taizé when a thirty-six-year-old woman from Romania pulled out a knife and slit the throat of the ninety-year-old founder. He died within minutes. Brother Roger Louis Schutz-Marsauche had sheltered refugees, including Jews, during the Nazi occupation, finally fleeing his home in Switzerland. After the war he was joined by others who shared his vision of a contemplative spiritual reconciliation. In 1940, he founded the community of Taizé.

During the 1950s, a particular ministry to youth was established. Since those days, literally hundreds of thousands of young people, as well as adults, have visited, stayed, studied, worshiped, and prayed as part of the community. Today there are over one hundred brothers and sisters representing both Roman Catholic and Protestant traditions. Out of the community arose scripture-based worship music that emphasizes the full participation of the gathered community. This simple music captures the quiet, reflective, prayerful spirit of worship at Taizé.

"Christ of compassion, you enable us to be in communion with those who have gone before us, and who can remain so close to us. We confide into your hands our Brother Roger. He already contemplates the invisible. In his footsteps, you are preparing us to welcome a radiance of your brightness. Brother Roger, with love and affection we entrust your blessed soul to the love and mercy of Almighty God; in the sure and certain hope of resurrection to eternal life. Amen."

—Prayer of the Community after Brother Roger's Death

Moments of Devotion

May I walk with eyes wide open, so that when the moment dawns, I recognize that which I am seeking.

Some Things to Think About

- What are your usual practices of prayer? Do you have daily disciplined ways of praying? Why or why not?
- How do you pray? What is one of the more common ways you pray? What ways do you pray that are "off the beaten track"?

Good and upright is the LORD;
   therefore he instructs sinners in the way.
He leads the humble in what is right,
   and teaches the humble his way.
All the paths of the LORD *are steadfast love and faithfulness,*
   for those who keep his covenant and his decrees.
                                        (Psalm 25:8-10)

❧ Day 20: The Sacrament of Place

Two paths converge in the making of a pilgrimage: the actual and the spiritual, the specific destination and the perpetual journey. The spiritual is not detached from the physical. Both pursue more than mere existence. Both require one to leave home. Both require discomfort and sleeping away from one's familiar bed.

I think of this pilgrimage I am taking as "exteriorized spirituality," the personal, spiritual journey made public. It is an act of my spiritual reality as well as a concrete journey, a physically enacted journey toward the Spirit.

Early sojourners did not see pilgrimage as a light task. They suffered the heat of the days and the cold of the nights. Kneeling, prostrating, and crawling on their knees brought bodily injury. Beyond all of this was the pressure that the pilgrims placed upon themselves to make sure they were traveling with purity of heart. They were steadfast in their fasting, prayer, and meditation. To struggle with holy abstractions while journeying from site to site was toilsome indeed.

As I reach my destination, I follow the custom of the pilgrim by bowing and saluting the ground with a kiss. In this first blushing kiss I pour out my gratitude. Physically kissing the ground or praying in front of a Mary statue was viewed by the sixteenth-century Protestant movement as pure superstition and idolatry. They viewed such actions as part of a cult manipulated for the prosperity of the church hierarchy. Of course, in some ways this was true. But they missed the point. As Christ the incarnate emphasizes, we humans need the physical—a physical place to stand, holy ground, to experience the sacred. As Anne Dumoulin writes, "Our first and most obvious discovery is that the pilgrimage is a *spatial prayer*. Of course, all our activities are situated in time and space. But it is clear that the pilgrim's way of proceeding would be meaningless if it were not a real journey to a holy place, recognized in space as a 'centre.'"[19]

The veneration of holy places is a primordial religious experience. Even Moses took off his shoes on holy ground. Some places are radically different because they are closer to God.

It is paradoxical that I should claim God is everywhere but seek God in special places, yet it is this paradox that my gut-level intuition accepts. Traveling to the Holy helps me to reflect on that which mediates holiness and thus, ultimately, to reflect on God. These encounters are impregnated with certain common spiritual experiences, and with the simple testimony of the many who have been helped spiritually by being in the presence of that which is felt to be holy.

There is a strange relationship between the spiritual and the physical. When we challenge the physical dimension by denying our usual tendency to indulge in the desires of our body, we can allow the spiritual space within us to grow. In the Middle Ages, pilgrims experienced many dangers, difficulties, and hardships, yet the toil of their journey enabled them to identify with the suffering of Christ.

I'm not sure that this has been researched and proven, this connection between hardship and spiritual growth, this "mortification of the flesh," as early Christians referred to it. But I have seen the growth of the spirit in such circumstances.

Moments of Devotion

May I take off my shoes when I reach holy ground so as not to miss the closeness of God.

Some Things to Think About

* As Christ the incarnate emphasizes, we humans need the physical—a physical place to stand, holy ground—to experience the sacred. In what physical space have you experienced the sacred?
* The veneration of holy places is a primordial religious experience. Even Moses took off his shoes on holy ground. On what "holy ground" have you found yourself humbled and obedient?

Vindicate me, O LORD,
  for I have walked in my integrity,
  and I have trusted in the LORD *without wavering.*
Prove me, O LORD, *and try me;*
  test my heart and mind.
For your steadfast love is before my eyes,
  and I walk in faithfulness to you. (Psalm 26:1-3)

❧ Day 21: Walking

Our group travels today by bus. Even as I am bounced along by the springs of the vehicle, I sense that the Holy is best approached by foot. The path needs to be traversed slowly, by walking. A slower pace allows the heart to catch up with the body.

A pilgrim's walk is not simply a matter of traveling to this shrine or that cathedral—or to some sacred or ordinary place near home. It is a deliberate surrender of routines and habits, leaving convenience and comfort behind. I am not a tourist whose aim is to see sights and travel in comfort. Tourists want to relax, not to be put upon or inconvenienced. I, as pilgrim, break with this preconception and, putting all my trust in God, set out on a quest that is inward as much as outward. I step literally into the unknown.

I would like to return in the future, if it is in God's grace, to travel by foot next time. Such thoughts come to me as I walk up to the cathedral door. "The God that the Bible proclaims reveals himself to be the holy God," Japanese theologian Kosuke Koyama writes. "He reveals himself to be holy by becoming slow for us."[20]

Just as earlier people walked and prayed, I do likewise. I approach the Holy slowly, hesitantly, with respect and humility. This pilgrimage provides me time to think of my past and time to think of the future. Walking, by its very nature, purges the body of toxins and clears the mind of mental muddle. This walk distills my thoughts so that all the "stuff" that has been obscuring clarity now rises to the top and floats away.

Walking is an essential part of my spiritual exploration. Early in the morning I put on my walking shoes and begin again to tread the earth from which I am made, the earth from which so often in my suburban life I am cut off. My feet hit the cobblestones, choppy grass, and hundreds of stairs, and I feel the beauty of God's creation. The rest of my body is busy too. My eyes see birds new to me for the first time; my nose smells the blooming lilacs. I listen to the fountain. At the end of the day, I am tired and my calves ache. I have the taste of sweat and hard work in my mouth. But through all this, and only all this, do I sense the change coming over me. A new song grows inside, a deeper harmony. The pilgrimage is at work.

Moments of Devotion

May I slow my pace and allow my heart to catch up with my body so that a new song might grow in my heart.

Some Things to Think About

- How does your body "speak" to let you know where you are on your spiritual journey? in your relationship with others? in your relationship with God?
- What routines and habits do you need to deliberately surrender in order to put all your trust in God and set out on a quest—that is as much inward as outward—to step literally into the unknown?

Hear my cry, O God;
listen to my prayer.
From the end of the earth I call to you,
when my heart is faint.
Lead me to the rock
that is higher than I;
for you are my refuge,
a strong tower against the enemy.
Let me abide in your tent forever,
find refuge under the shelter of your wings. (Psalm 61:1-4)

❧ Day 22: Healing Peace

"A pilgrim is a wanderer with a purpose," says Peace Pilgrim. She explains:

> A pilgrimage can be to a place—that's the best-known kind—but it can also be for a thing. Mine is for peace, and that is why I am Peace Pilgrim. . . .
> The situation in the world around us is just a reflection of the collective situation. In the final analysis, only as we become more peaceful people will we be finding ourselves living in a more peaceful world. [21]

We've all taken to the road with causes and hopes. Some pilgrims, like Peace Pilgrim, walk for justice or hope of a better future while others walk for health.

A Wandering Peace Pilgrim

From 1953 to 1981 a silver-haired woman calling herself only "Peace Pilgrim" walked more than 25,000 miles in the U.S. on a personal pilgrimage for peace. She vowed to "remain a wanderer until mankind has learned the way of peace, walking until . . . given shelter and fasting until . . . given food."[22]

Many of the early pilgrims also took up the journey looking for health. It was a last hope for the chronically sick and maimed. They would travel from one holy site to the next until they felt sufficiently cured. A few moved about for many years. When eventually they would receive a cure, one of the holy places would be credited. Others would choose to visit three sites by casting lots or drawing straws. Since God was ultimately in charge of life and death, sickness and health, they saw their cure not as dumb luck but as divine intervention.[23]

Pilgrimage by Proxy

Palmers were paid surrogates who took pilgrimages for rich clients. Pilgrimage by proxy was common. Professional pilgrims who carried a ring or rosary in the name of the sponsor, touching it to the holy shrine, visited cherished sites. Some readily took up the mendicant life for the sake of adventure to foreign lands.[24]

Regardless of the reason for their journey, many pilgrims in the Middle Ages were anxious to prove themselves bona fide pilgrims. So to distinguish themselves from other travelers, tradesmen, or even robbers who often would dress as pilgrims or priests, they made sure that an emblem was prominently displayed. The most famous insignia was the Saint James shell gathered on the beaches of Galicia when in Compostela.

The other day we met a real pilgrim. He was dressed in brown, with a large scallop shell tied by leather straps around his neck. The Jerusalem Community at Vézelay welcomed him by way of the morning office with prayers and then sent him on his way with a loaf of bread, the common tribute to the hungry pilgrim.

I spoke to him briefly afterward. He is a priest, about my own age. He set out during Holy Week and hopes to arrive in Spain on July 25, the Feast of Saint James. He is walking the ancient route to Santiago. I wish I were. I feel like an impostor calling myself a pilgrim, riding in this modern, motorized vehicle. Yet, like him, I am on a journey, anxiously searching, looking for a new beginning, for a fundamental healing. I say this to him. He smiles at me and says that pilgrimage is not about how one gets there. It is about an attitude of openness to the Spirit. Pilgrimage is what happens when one waits—with open heart and mind—for God.

Today I sit in the Le Puy church at the feet of the Black Madonna and remember the priest's words. During the fifth century, Christians found this to be a place where the Spirit of God worked miracles and healing. By the sixth century, the numbers had grown so huge that a hospice was built.

I am not at all willing to set aside such stories as wild tales. I'm trusting in this eternal phenomenon that has remained through the centuries. I am proud to stand alongside women like Peace Pilgrim and say that I want to be healed too, and I invite the world to come along.

Moments of Devotion

May I take on an attitude of openness to the Spirit and wait—with openness of heart and mind—for God.

Some Things to Think About

- Is God calling you to be on a pilgrimage for a "thing"? Peace Pilgrim's pilgrimage was for peace. Perhaps your pilgrimage is for peace, or restoration of the earth, or food for all children. What is your pilgrimage *for*?
- When have you felt like an impostor, and how did that feeling hamper your openness to the Spirit?

Who shall ascend the hill of the LORD?
And who shall stand in his holy place?
Those who have clean hands and pure hearts,
   who do not lift up their souls to what is false,
   and do not swear deceitfully.
They will receive blessing from the LORD,
   and vindication from the God of their salvation.
Such is the company of those who seek him,
   who seek the face of the God of Jacob. (Psalm 24:3-6)

❧ Day 23: Devotion

My intention is not to see Chartres or Taizé in order to boast "I've been there" or "I've seen that," as tempting as that seems at times. This is a pilgrimage of prayer. I am seeking to be in the presence of God, which is the essence of prayer. My first objective is not to see the sights of the Black Virgin or the relics of Mary Magdalene, but to kiss the ground and give thanks and then to pray and venerate the Holy in this place.

I go as a devotion. Devotions are not what one reads or prays, but what one does. I live my devoutness by going on pilgrimage, participating in the line processions, joining in the worship and singing, wearing travel clothes, and performing other meaningful rituals.

I reflect on the fourteenth-century writings of Margery Kempe, who grew "anxious of becoming proud and vainglorious." She records Christ's assuring words:

> Daughter, do not be afraid, I shall take away your pride. And those who honor you, honor me; they that despise you, despise me, and I will punish them. I am in you, and you in me. And those who do listen to you hear the voice of God. Daughter, if any living person, no matter how sinful he might have been will leave his sin and listen to what you tell him, I will show my love for you by giving him whatever grace you promise I will give him.[25]

At one time I would have thought taking a pilgrimage to be simpleminded, fanatical, or theologically naive. Those thoughts are now vanquished. It is enough that I am here in this timeless, holy space. There is no room for hesitation, critical appraisal, or cynical judgment. I inhale it all and am transported by my fervor and the devotion of the moment—even to the extent of seeing Christ in the midst.

Moments of Devotion

May I seek to be in the presence of God, which is the essence of prayer.

Some Things to Think About

- Perhaps at one time you thought that taking a pilgrimage or engaging in other religious rituals was simpleminded, fanatical, or theologically naive. If so, how has your opinion changed?
- If modern-day devotions are not what one reads or prays but what one does, what devotion have you practiced today?

How weighty to me are your thoughts, O God!
    How vast is the sum of them!
I try to count them—they are more than the sand;
    I come to the end—I am still with you.
O that you would kill the wicked, O God,
    and that the bloodthirsty would depart from me—
those who speak of you maliciously,
    and lift themselves up against you for evil!
Do I not hate those who hate you, O LORD?
    And do I not loathe those who rise up against you?
I hate them with perfect hatred;
    I count them my enemies.
Search me, O God, and know my heart;
    test me and know my thoughts.
See if there is any wicked way in me,
    and lead me in the way everlasting. (Psalm 139:17-24)

❧ Day 24: Repentance

The movement of repentance is strong within me. I struggle to make God's will the guiding principle of my life. I struggle to love the unlovable. I struggle to step outside myself and know that I am not the center of the universe. I struggle to love the people on this trip. There is so much within me that needs to be opened up and cleansed by the Holy Spirit.

In *The Study of Spirituality* we read, "The pilgrim seeks to assist this inner change partly by contemplating the figure of Christ, partly by a self-examination which seeks to uncover the disordered emotions and desires which need to be cleansed and redirected."[26] This is my opportunity to see myself as I truly am. That is what the Holy Spirit does. A mirror is held up for us to gaze into.

Daily I ask for forgiveness and love to cover my missteps. I did not come on this pilgrimage to be a tour host. I came as a spiritual guide to offer group spiritual direction and, when helpful, individual support and encouragement. This is a pilgrimage of prayer and nothing more, yet nothing less. The bit of tourism thrown in is distracting to me. What a strange mixture is all that we have experienced so far. Some pilgrims buy souvenirs. Strange how religious trinkets intermingle with profound meditation.

Today we prayed at the chapel of Le Puy, a place known for healing. I was anointed with chrism, consecrated oil, for the healing of my spirit and body and as a symbol of the salvation of my soul. I feel that I need to be anointed and prayed for daily, for I am so sinful. My mind reminds me that nothing can separate me from God's love, but my heart still seeks assurance. I long for the Eucharist daily and to pray by the hour once reaching a holy place. I want to use all the means of grace that are open to me for my healing on this pilgrimage. For me, this pilgrimage is about prayer—praying without ceasing.

To walk as a pilgrim is to pray with each step.

Moments of Devotion

May I prayerfully step outside myself in order to be opened up and cleansed by the Holy Spirit.

Some Things to Think About

• What is there within you that needs to be opened up and cleansed by the Holy Spirit? What do you seek to assist this inner change?

• Pilgrimage is about prayer—about praying without ceasing. To walk as a pilgrim is to pray with each step. What disciplines of prayer walk with you each and every day?

I was glad when they said to me,
    "Let us go to the house of the LORD!"
Our feet are standing
    within your gates, O Jerusalem. (Psalm 122:1-2)

❧ Day 25: Community

I've chosen good company for this journey. Or, the truth be told, it was they who chose to accompany me. I'm not saying that everything is always perfect or that there aren't moments when I wish I were traveling in solitude. The church is not a place of sweetness and light. This working out our salvation with fear and trembling is very messy business indeed! We may not have had to face, as did the pilgrims in post-Roman days, nasty toll-collectors or brigades on the highway. But we have already contended with street gypsies who got away with a wallet. And we contend with one another—imperfect vessels for such a journey.

Nineteenth-century Danish philosopher and theologian Søren Kierkegaard must have taken a pilgrimage with a group at some time, for he wrote, "It is terrible how boring the conversation generally is when people have to be so long together as we are now. Just as toothless folk have to turn the food round and round in their mouths, so the same remark gets repeated over and over again, till the last one has to spit it out."[27]

Let me balance Kierkegaard's remark with one written by Hadewijch, a thirteenth-century Beguine mystic:

> Closely observe, with regard either to myself or to others in whom you seek sincere practice of virtue, who they are that help you to improve, and consider what their life is. For there are all too few on earth today in whom you can find true fidelity; for almost all people now want from God and men what pleases them and what they desire or lack.[28]

Despite awkward moments, I, like Hadewijch, feel I am with holy lovers of God, people who love and honor the Divine. Our hearts are united and elevated toward God. Therefore, I trust this small band of pilgrims to help me move into greater awareness of the Holy. When they speak, I listen intently, and I see them in serenity listening to me. I learn the most about God from my friends.

The word *parish* comes from the Greek *paraikos*. It means "pilgrim" or "passing stranger." With our hands stretched across the table, we bless the food with another passing stranger. Like Jesus, we break the bread, we drop our masks, and we discover truth. We live open to the discovery of what being the church is all about. Is this not the true meaning of the Christian pilgrimage? Isn't this what pilgrimage is about—to catch a glimpse of the future city of God already breaking into our present?

Ours is not a pilgrimage that takes shortcuts, that seeks to experience prematurely the fullness of communion. But it is the breaking down of barriers, a step toward life as God intends, a foot into a church that works. This is *koinonia*, "community."

In whispers we break the bread in a side chapel of the cathedral, waiting for the "Protestant police" to come and arrest us. We are committed to the unity of Christians, and we long for the day when we will be invited to stand as one at the Eucharistic table. We are grounded in our own tradition; still, we reach across the aisle to experience as fully as possible the liturgy and prayer of others who worship the same God who is present to each of us. We share this pilgrimage lifestyle with others also on this path. We hope that because we do this in the present, we take one step closer to setting one another free. Committed to the corporate life of the church, we share as we are able.

Here we are, pilgrim people on our way to the promised land, travelers who not long ago were strangers to one another. Now we pray together and share our lives. Together we feel joyful in Jesus Christ. Here we shed our shyness and are born in this new view of life. The grace of God enables us to "rejoice with those who rejoice, weep with those who weep. Live in harmony with one another" (Romans 12:15-16). We reach out to one another, beyond the barriers that usually separate us, and risk encountering God.

This strange broken sense of community underlies our pilgrimage. We approach a shrine in an act of corporate thanksgiving. We light a candle as a community act of tribute and devotion. Together we see salvation and healing, not solely for individuals but for the whole community, which we sense is an expansion of our personal lives. Each of us has personal reasons for making the journey, but we all share a collective view that our pilgrimage will benefit the entire community to which we will return.

Moments of Devotion

May I remember that I share this journey with holy lovers of God so that my heart, with theirs, may be united and elevated toward God.

Some Things to Think About

- When have you experienced a healing community where hearts are united and elevated toward God? And when have you experienced broken community?
- How committed are you to the corporate life of the church?

Happy is everyone who fears the LORD,
who walks in his ways. (Psalm 128:1)

☙ Day 26: Journaling

I leave my travel journal behind in the pew and discover it missing only after I am on the bus. Sick at heart, I retrace my steps into the dimness of the cathedral. At first I feel anxious. Then I think of this: no anxiety must ever rule me. No loss is irredeemable. Even death is not a real disaster, as it is the one certain event in life. Why worry? It is only a diary, a vapor of pen to paper, less than important. But I'm relieved all the same when my book of notes and reflections is safely back in my coat pocket.

I had just penned this poem. It might have been lost.

> Divine Wisdom, today I walk on the cobbles
>   where earlier pilgrims walked.
> I touch the stone floor of the crypt.
> I see the standing stones of the resting faithful.
> I stand in the rays of your Eastern light at the altar
>   illuminated by the warmth that touches my face.
> I visit the altar where they prayed,
> And sit by the city wall where they rested.
> I feel their presence and hear their witness.
> Be with me now as I continue my earthly pilgrimage
>   to the New Jerusalem where every tear will be
>   wiped away,
>   and I will be with you forever.

"I think you will hear a message from God telling you who you are now to be," Mary had said to me on a previous day of travel. This comment had surprised me, compelling me to look deeper. Now that I am at the end of my pilgrimage, I see the truth in it. And I thank God. I am no longer perplexed; this pilgrimage has opened me to hope and expectation. I still don't know where I am going, of course; none of us knows. Jesus tells me that we cannot know the way we are going. But he whispers reassuringly to me, and this is life.

I am at peace.

Moments of Devotion

May I let go of all expectations, hear the whispers of my Lord, and be at peace.

Some Things to Think About

- "Divine Wisdom" seems to name this one I call God. What other names for God might you use that define your relationship?
- Do you use a spiritual journal? If so, how do you use it to further your walk with God?

PART THREE:
HOME IS THE JOURNEY

Let my cry come before you, O LORD;
give me understanding according to your word.
Let my supplication come before you;
deliver me according to your promise. (Psalm 119:169-170)

❧ Day 27: It Is Finished

In many ways I am your average traveler. Like pilgrims past, I have walked the walk, and now, transformed and renewed, I want to return home as quickly as possible. I push my seat on the plane into a reclining position, pull down the window shade, and envision my own bed and pillow. Just as I had to prepare for the pilgrimage, I suddenly realize that I now need to prepare to move into my future life. Life lived with God, in God, and through God. I am about to doze off when my mind begins to run through the experiences of these past thirteen days. They were so full of wonder, frustration, charm, and trial that I thought they would never end. Now I settle back into my seat on this last leg of my voyage and say, "Well, it is finished."

I've moved many times through the years, each time leaving family and the friends acquired over a span of my life. It seems that each decade I move to a region where I know nobody and, worse, where nobody knows me. At first I am blue. Then I begin to feel new joy and sweet promise that life can be reinvented. I am part of something greater than myself and part of a ministry that really matters.

But in some cases, somehow it all goes sour. There is a sunken heart in the middle of me. I become too brittle, too defended, too pockmarked by life. My rational mind, that voice that speaks in public places, tells me that I am the victim of circumstances. The job becomes bankrupt, my coworkers or boss change, and the job I thought I was hired for evaporates with corporate changes. It is as if there is a cosmic convergence that shatters my carefully constructed life. The other voice inside my head, the one that speaks in the dark of night, tells me it is all my fault, that I have a fatal flaw, that it was right for me to be set aside, that I am not worth much to others and perhaps even to God.

So it was good to pack my bag and escape to a far-off place for a time. I had planned this adventure back when I was still gainfully employed and had things figured out. I was making a difference.

There is now only the journey home. I muse sadly that my pilgrimage time has passed. My journey in France has come to an end. The realization plucks at my heartstrings. But the pilgrimage I began there will never end.

Moments of Devotion

May I thoughtfully examine my preconceived ideas about how life is supposed to be so that my happiness does not depend upon rigid conceptions.

Some Things to Think About

- Was there a time in your life when it was good to pack your bags and escape to a far-off place for a time? Where did you go? What did you do to renew your spirit?
- What cosmic convergences have shattered your carefully planned life? How did you feel as a victim of circumstances? How did you work through the chaos to come out on the other side?

*To you, O L*ORD*, I cried,*
  and to the LORD *I made supplication:*
"What profit is there in my death,
  if I go down to the Pit?
Will the dust praise you?
  Will it tell of your faithfulness?
Hear, O LORD*, and be gracious to me!*
  O LORD*, be my helper!"*
You have turned my mourning into dancing;
  you have taken off my sackcloth
  and clothed me with joy,
so that my soul may praise you and not be silent.
  O LORD *my God, I will give thanks to you forever.*
                                    (Psalm 30:8-12)

❧ Day 28: A Lighter Suitcase

A wise Trappist monk and spiritual guide, Thomas Merton, wrote, "I am going home, to a home where I have never been in this body, where I have never been in this washable suit (washed by Sister Gerarda the other day at the Redwoods), where I have never been with these suitcases."[29]

Healing and pilgrimage naturally fit together. In times of great personal devastation, I have searched for a center around which I could reimagine my life. In that time of chaos, I longed for a transcendent center, a God who would bring about order and safety. My quest was an active search born of deep longing and trust that my desire would be honored at the end of my seeking. It was.

This time, now over twenty years later, I travel for a different reason: to validate myself as the same person I have known for years. My situation since the change in my employment has been one of grief and confusion. I am searching to reclaim my vocational identity. I remind myself that it is my baptism alone—my identity in Christ—that defines me. On this pilgrimage I want a restored sense of peacefulness, but what I find first is the catharsis of mourning. I face the process of grief, rather than denial. Deep within I know that if I can endure passage through this difficult period, I may find a new sense of well-being.

Thinking back, I unloaded a lot from my "suitcase" while traveling from place to place. At our first stop, Chartres, I left a piece of my anger, and at the second, on the hill of Mont Marie, I put off hopelessness. Finally, somewhere between Vézelay and Le Puy, out fell my sadness, and I decided to not pick it up but to leave it behind.

My facing the reality of loss and change helped me to accept my unknown future. This unsettling, turbulent trip was gracefully accompanied by a sense of emptying within my soul that made room for grace. As I return home, my "suitcase" is lighter. It has a new spaciousness in which to grow and become. I carry a new vision that remains with me even as I journey home. Only now can I begin to comfortably recite Psalm 30, "You have turned my mourning into dancing" (v. 11).

Moments of Devotion

May I, in times of chaos and turbulence, empty my soul to make room for grace.

Some Things to Think About

- What would you like to unload from your "suitcase"? How about a piece of your anger or a bit of hopelessness or sadness?
- Now that you have left some of your baggage behind, what would you like to pick up along the way to help you make it home? What new vision would sustain you?

Let me hear what God the LORD will speak,
  for he will speak peace to his people,
  to his faithful, to those who turn to him in their hearts.
Surely his salvation is at hand for those who fear him,
  that his glory may dwell in our land.
Steadfast love and faithfulness will meet;
  righteousness and peace will kiss each other.

  (Psalm 85:8-10)

❧ Day 29: The Presence of Mary Magdalene

So there I was, a pilgrim on The Way, restless indeed, searching constantly for that which would make me fully and truly myself. And I discovered that it was only when I was peace, when I was love, when I was delighting in the beauty of the people and places around me that I was closest to being my most authentic self. I felt most authentically myself in the presence of the spirit of Mary Magdalene. Her story of audacious spirit as portrayed in the Gospels encourages me. In fact, I now claim her as my name-saint. The Gospel of Luke introduces "Mary from the town of Magdala in the Galilee, or Mejdel as it is known today.... She is important enough to be identified—an uncommon thing for women in male documents to begin with—and she is mentioned fourteen times. She is mentioned more times, in other words, than any other woman in the New Testament except Mary the mother of Jesus."[30]

I encountered Mary Magdalene first in Vézelay, where I saw her relics encased in a beautiful round tube of glass and gold. It was in the crypt. I heard a voice as I was kneeling, venerating the Blessed Sacrament. I can only call this hearing a mystery. It cannot be rationally explained. I almost melted at her sound. I couldn't pray without crying, and I knew that God was speaking through Mary to me—her spirit displayed in her ancient story now speaking to me. My heart was filled as if I was just stepping inside my home after being away for a lifetime.

In Veneration We Show Respect

Veneration, in Latin *veneratio*, is a special way to remember and honor a past saint who has lived and died in Christ. Through showing respect to their memory we honor God who made them and in whose image they are made. Veneration is often shown by respectfully bowing, kissing, or making the ancient sign of the cross in the place where the person once lived. Although we venerate their memory, only God alone is worshiped.

Moments of Devotion

May I open my heart to be filled with God's mysterious presence so that I may be fully and truly myself.

Some Things to Think About

- When have you felt God's mysterious presence? How did it move your spirit to be a more authentic you?
- Read again and encounter the story of Mary Magdalene in the Scriptures. What is the message of her story to you?

I lift up my eyes to the hills—
from where will my help come?
My help comes from the LORD,
who made heaven and earth.
He will not let your foot be moved;
he who keeps you will not slumber.
He who keeps Israel
will neither slumber nor sleep.
The LORD *is your keeper;*
the LORD *is your shade at your right hand.*
The sun shall not strike you by day,
nor the moon by night.
The LORD *will keep you from all evil;*
he will keep your life.
The LORD *will keep*
your going out and your coming in
from this time on and forevermore. (Psalm 121)

❧ Day 30: Pray for Us Sinners

I kneel on the floor, hours on end, with my rosary in hand. I begin my mantra of Hail Marys, this time skipping over the Lord's Prayer and other in-between stuff without guilt. After about a zillion beads, I am open to pray.

How have I deserved such gracious and kind people throughout my life? I've been blessed all my days with generosity—and all I notice is what is missing. Am I like the woman in a novel I once read? The woman hated her home and had completely forgotten about the love of her children. She was determined to believe that the world was an unfriendly and very disappointing place. Like her, I've been refusing to notice what I've been given.

Mother Eve's story is poignant in this moment. God gave her everything. About only one thing did God say, "Do not touch." And Eve's eyes moved from all that she had to what she was missing. It is the human condition. Inner turmoil begins at the moment that I become blind to what I have and see only what I lack. Am I conditioned to believe that I need more to be content? It isn't bad to have more. It is bad when I cannot see what I do have.

Since returning home I've talked this over with a friend. "It makes perfect sense," she says. "If you are focused on what you don't have, you are in a constant state of craving. It's the same as seeing the glass half empty. You see what you don't have instead of what you have." In that moment, dissatisfaction began to evaporate.

I'd been missing the beauty of the landscape all around me by focusing on the sun, which I could not get to. I'd been so blinded with my own disillusionment that I'd almost missed the view when I'd finally reached it. This was not the first time. I shamefully admit that I've caught myself doing this many times before—this seeing the glass half empty. I've caught myself and promised not to do it again. I have done this even though I know that the journey itself is everything. "Mary, Mother of God, pray for us sinners, now."

Moments of Devotion

May I see the beauty of the landscape and know that the journey itself is everything.

Some Things to Think About

- What kind of person are you? Do you see your glass half empty or half full? How is your outlook on life working for you?
- Why not go for a walk around your house or neighborhood or building and take stock of the beauty all around you? With new eyes and a renewed heart, look at people, designs, art, and nature. It is all beautiful.

Happy are the people who know the festal shout,
who walk, O LORD, *in the light of your countenance;*
they exult in your name all day long,
and extol your righteousness.
For you are the glory of their strength;
by your favor our horn is exalted. (Psalm 89:15-17)

❧ Day 31: Hail Mary

I fall into bed exhausted on my first night home and then find myself wide awake at 3:00 a.m. I click on the light. On my bed stand are the prayer beads that traveled with me on pilgrimage.

I pick them up again. They are now so familiar in my hands. I place the cool, shiny cross upon my forehead—"In the name of the Father"—touch it to my chest—"and of the Son"—and then move it quickly, shoulder to shoulder—"and of the Holy Spirit. Amen." I hastily ramble through the Creed. Fingering the first bead, I recite the Lord's Prayer. The truth is hard to admit to myself, a dyed-in-the-wool Protestant—I can hardly wait for the Hail Marys! "Hail Mary, full of grace, the Lord is with thee. Blessed art thou amongst women and blessed is the fruit of thy womb, Jesus. Holy Mary, mother of God, pray for us sinners now and at the hour of our death. Amen."

I'd taken the rosary along as part of the designated pilgrimage garb. I tied it around my waist; the longer-than-usual string worked well for the purpose. I found the beads handy in my right-hand pocket. I could finger them unnoticed. Somehow their touch gave me comfort. Reassurance. I felt that I was not on this journey alone—that Mary was with me.

Mary suffered, and we remember her for that; but that is not what we most celebrate her for. Mary suffered the way all people do, and she survived the suffering without becoming embittered by it; she survived it with love. She is not a martyr, and she invites us to find refuge in her heart—that famous heart she wears on her breast in the pictures.

I carry Mary with me all the time now. She is in my heart, in the air that I breathe. I want to share her with others and tell everyone whom I've found. For the first time I understand why people proselytize. I am happy. I have found a way. I want to share it so that others can find the way too. But now that I am home, I control my impulse. I show my rosary and with restraint say, "I've found praying the rosary a new center for my prayer life. I know—it is hard to believe." One woman rolls her eyes. I hardly care.

I read that there are those who believe that the Holy Spirit is Mary. I do know that Mary received the gift of the Holy Spirit on the day of Pentecost. It was the Holy Spirit who placed the kindled flame on the heads of believers; who gives guidance and truth. I've come to believe that the Father, Son, and Holy Spirit are the face of God—and Mary, too, shows us a different face of God, or Love, in the world. I picture each member of the Trinity at different times when I pray. And I also remember Mary. I am strongly drawn to this feminine hero of the faith—a compassionate, gentle, soft woman. Yes, it is Mary's story that inspires me on my way home. Hail, Mary.

Moments of Devotion

May I survive suffering without becoming embittered by it; may I survive it with compassion.

Some Things to Think About

- Do you have a special Bible, cross, beads, or other object that you hold onto when praying? If so, what does it represent to you? How does it aid your prayer?
- Which story about Mary most touches your heart? How does Mary's story inspire and encourage you?

Where can I go from your spirit?
Or where can I flee from your presence?
If I ascend to heaven, you are there;
    if I make my bed in Sheol, you are there.
If I take the wings of the morning
    and settle at the farthest limits of the sea,
even there your hand shall lead me,
    and your right hand shall hold me fast.
If I say, "Surely the darkness shall cover me,
    and the light around me become night,"
even the darkness is not dark to you;
    the night is as bright as the day,
    for darkness is as light to you. (Psalm 139:7-12)

✒ Day 32: Homecoming: A Love Story

The pilgrim's way runs through the whole gospel, and the supper is the homecoming point of the love story. One might say that the Eucharist was born of a pilgrimage. Jesus went with the crowd to Jerusalem as a participant in the Passover pilgrimage. Integral to Jewish faith and practice was the holy obligation prescribed by the Torah for all Jewish males "to go up" to Jerusalem three times a year for the festivals of Passover, Weeks, and Tabernacles. But, as Christopher Lewis, dean of Christ Church, writes, "God is to be worshipped anywhere and if he is to be met, the meeting is first and foremost in those in need and in the sacraments, not in places of any particular kind."[31]

One hope that I carried for our needy community was that we would celebrate the sacrament of the Eucharist daily. Although I imagined us lifting the cup in great cathedrals and humble monasteries, one day we celebrated outside the church gates, unable to gain entrance. Everyone was not always present at these celebrations, but that was not the point. This prayer of great thanksgiving is raised in places both grand and lowly, with a few individuals or the whole community. This bread and wine is God's action toward us, not our actions toward God. It is God's work, not our work.

Likewise, when the evening or morning liturgies were prayed by one or two, they prayed for the entire body, knowing that each individual was participating, some praying in secret. Each person in his or her own way joined along with the heavenly host. Those who partook in the time of adoration or celebration did so on behalf of all. "For where two or three are gathered in my name, I am there among them" (Matthew 18:20).

Moments of Devotion

May I embrace the sacraments, creating a welcoming place for all others, even as I make possible my own spiritual transformation.

Some Things to Think About

- "God is to be worshipped anywhere and if he is to be met, the meeting is first and foremost in those in need and in the sacraments, not in places of any particular kind" (Christopher Lewis). Name the poor who have helped you meet God.
- How have the sacraments of Baptism and Eucharist—Holy Communion—been instrumental in your faith journey?

O LORD, you have searched me and known me.
You know when I sit down and when I rise up;
you discern my thoughts from far away.
You search out my path and my lying down,
and are acquainted with all my ways.
Even before a word is on my tongue,
O LORD, you know it completely.
You hem me in, behind and before,
and lay your hand upon me.
Such knowledge is too wonderful for me;
it is so high that I cannot attain it. (Psalm 139:1-6)

❧ Day 33: Rules for Pilgrimage?

On this once-in-a-lifetime pilgrimage to France, I thought that I could build spaciousness where the Spirit was at work and that a Christ community would emerge and flourish. At the end of the pilgrimage, I came home with both sharp judgment and profound hope.

The best-case scenario for pilgrimages is that they have a flexible itinerary rather than a schedule. The only way to make a true pilgrimage is to do it with an open end. In our case, this was not possible. Nevertheless, next time (if there is a next time) I will build in more flexibility and "down time," and plan to stay in one place at least two to three nights to allow our souls to catch up with our bodies.

The problem was not the number of travelers or an insufficiency to meet our basic needs. We had what we needed. I heard grumbling, though rarely directly. We needed a better guide (ours was sick with an ear infection most of the trip) and a better-arranged program (some planned sites did not work out). A few thought I was wanting, and I have to agree.

Now, some time later, my judgment is that the difficulty was none of these. Our problem was fundamentally theological. Our true mission as pilgrims was to be God's presence and work in the world. I had no inclination to be a tour host trying to meet the needs of religious "consumers." Instead, I expected to be a spiritual guide who would pastor the community to embody the reconciliation that God has planned for us and for all creation. I wanted us to live the fruit of the Spirit—love, joy, peace, patience, kindness, gentleness, and self-control. My vision of community was one of a "demonstration community" or "contrast society," encompassing a way of life, a set of expectations. I wanted to serve as a midwife to the Holy Spirit's work, so that we would then reflect Christ, even if imperfectly.

"Beloved, we are God's children now; what we will be has not yet been revealed. What we do know is this: when he is revealed, we will be like him, for we will see him as he is. And all who have this hope in him purify themselves, just as he is pure" (1 John 3:2-3). I truly believe this. I kept believing and waiting for that mystical moment when the Spirit would open the inner eye of our hearts and we would see the kingdom of God with clarity through the eyes of love. I saw that happen for a few; but for the group as a whole, that moment never came.

I now see that being Christ's community requires not only a change in communal life but also an examination of individual behavior. Changing the patterns of community life alone does not suffice. Perhaps there were too many individual agendas that superseded the obligations or commitment to the group. Perhaps preexisting relationships of family or friends were held in higher regard than the good and love of the total community. Most members of the group commented that physical limitations were the largest obstacle to the group becoming a community. Some members didn't adhere to the one-bag rule. Others simply were not in a physical condition to travel on a more strenuous pilgrimage venue.

Now, post-pilgrimage, I have many more questions than answers. I recognize that I was clueless. I do know that as the pilgrimage wore on, my prayer became a simple one—a prayer for well-being and for us to allow God to fill in the blanks.

Moments of Devotion

May I build spaciousness within my heart and actions where the Holy Spirit can be at work within me.

Some Things to Think About

- What is your true mission as a pilgrim? Is it to be God's presence and work in the world? If so, how are you living this reality? If not, why? How can you realign your life to take on a truly God-centered mission?
- Most of us want to live into the fruit of the Spirit—love, joy, peace, patience, kindness, gentleness, and self-control. Which aspect of the fruit do you need more of in your life?

O God, you are my God, I seek you,
  my soul thirsts for you;
my flesh faints for you,
  as in a dry and weary land where there is no water.
So I have looked upon you in the sanctuary,
  beholding your power and glory.
Because your steadfast love is better than life,
  my lips will praise you.
So I will bless you as long as I live;
  I will lift up my hands and call on your name. (Psalm 63:1-4)

🐦 Day 34: The "Next Time" Pilgrim

On the trip home, I began to write down some "musts" for myself when on pilgrimage. With a more relaxed and humble heart, I began to journal my reflections, which are now before you in the form of this book. These are for me. I hope that you, the reader, will keep what speaks to your heart and leave the rest.

Next time I am on pilgrimage, I will let go of preconceived notions about the trip and simply pick up my pilgrim's staff. I don't want to insist on having food or worship "just like we do back home." For instance, I learned how to eat in a new way: a leisurely two hours of wine-filled conversation. And I learned how to live at a new pace: slower and more contemplative, and in keeping with the business and resting hours of the culture. Some churches were closed from twelve to two when our bus arrived. Once I got locked in a crypt when the guard left for ten minutes, and I missed the first ten minutes of evening prayer in the basilica. Such experiences were blessings in disguise for they caused me to stop my hurried attitude.

Although we were in a new place with fresh circumstances, we still had the tendency to mimic the dominant American culture back home—a tendency that bears little resemblance to the reign of God in Jesus Christ. Reflecting these values and attitudes had the effect of inhibiting us from traveling in faith or even being witnesses to one another.

Our pilgrimage stretched the routines of the locals too. Our bus driver had never driven to Taizé before. He told us that he also had never, never left a group in the red light district of Paris and that he did so now in fear and disbelief. Later I overheard one member of our troop say to another, "This is not like other tours I've been on. They were better organized." She was right. I was aiming for a process, not perfection. A pilgrimage is not a tour. A pilgrimage happens to you as you go along. That is the wonder of it. It is an adventure to see what will be around the next bend that will delight or overwhelm. It is an experience that truly has never been done this way before. This pilgrimage was, indeed, unique.

Moments of Devotion

May I forget about perfection and be ready for the unusual and open to the wonder of the new.

Some Things to Think About

- A pilgrimage happens to you as you go along. That is the wonder of it. When and where have you experienced this kind of wonder?
- How might you break away from a life that mimics the dominant American culture? What would it look like?

Protect me, O God, for in you I take refuge.
I say to the LORD, *"You are my Lord;*
  I have no good apart from you."
As for the holy ones in the land, they are the noble,
  in whom is all my delight. (Psalm 16:1-3)

❧ Day 35: Angels Travel Lightly

The next time I go on pilgrimage, I'll travel light. I won't take excessive emotional or physical baggage but will go as an empty vessel ready to receive both spiritually and physically. My motto will be: Be open to wonder.

A few of our participants, including my husband, thought they were only tourists. At the end of the trip they, along with my spouse, told me with amazement how they had been touched at a particular crypt or shrine. Their desire for wholeness (like the word *holiness*) drew them to a certain place rather than to others. For some, the search was an effort to repair what was broken, to find again a dream that was lost, or to find clarity in what had been vague. Others, like myself, sought healing.

We became pilgrims as we opened ourselves to the power of prayer. And our prayers were answered. We rediscovered the balance between active accomplishment and intentional, quiet reflection. I rate the inner contemplative movement as equal in importance to the physical journey. Better yet is the combination of outward and inner seeking. Both require the journey.

Moments of Devotion

May I travel light and be open to wonder so that I may be healed.

Some Things to Think About

- What excessive emotional or physical baggage do you need to leave behind in order to become an empty vessel ready to receive both spiritually and physically?
- One motto is "Be open to wonder." What is your motto?

135

You who have made me see many troubles and calamities
will revive me again;
from the depths of the earth
you will bring me up again.
You will increase my honor,
and comfort me once again. *(Psalm 71:20-21)*

❧ Day 36: The Winding Road

The next time I'm on pilgrimage, I'll remember that walking the walk involves sacrifice. There are 328 steps from the crypt to the dome of Mont Marie in Paris, and those were only the beginning of the steps I'd climb. This is what makes a pilgrimage different from a vacation at the beach. If you work hard for something, you appreciate it more. Next time I'll expect a blister and a few bumps and bruises.

Next time I'll walk with other pilgrims along the way. The spirit of camaraderie is quite evident in the way we interact with others on pilgrimage. For Jesus, the pilgrimage was his destiny; and so it is for us. We walk with others on the way. Through having shared prayer and *lectio divina* (a slow, contemplative reading of the Scriptures), gracing one another at meals, and helping others, we come to experience our pilgrimage as part of the Lord's community. This is a community where God lives and where people love God—a people with roots in a simple piety.

Next time I'll remember that I'm not the center of the universe. Everything is not about me. I am a part of a community. The church is the creation of the Spirit. Jesus' disciples had but one heart and one soul, and they had all their property in common, owning nothing individually. On a plane or bus or in a shared room, we too hold all things in common and travel with one heart and one soul. To do otherwise is not in keeping with the spirit of our journey.

Is it not true that goods shared in common are worth so much more than goods owned by individuals? Can we exceed one another in well doing? It is worth a try.

Christina Rossetti, English poet of the nineteenth century, writes about the community in pilgrimage in her poem "Up-Hill."

> Does the road wind up-hill all the way?
> Yes, to the very end.
> Will the day's journey take the whole long day?
> From morn to night, my friend.
> But is there for the night a resting-place?
> A roof for when the slow dark hours begin.
> May not the darkness hide it from my face?
> You cannot miss that inn.

Shall I meet other wayfarers at night?
  Those who have gone before.
Then must I knock, or call when just in sight?
  They will not keep you standing at that door.

Shall I find comfort, travel-sore and weak?
  Of labor you shall find the sum.
Will there be beds for me and all who seek?
  Yea, beds for all who come.[32]

Moments of Devotion

May I walk with fellow pilgrims along the way to experience the wonderful camaraderie of community.

Some Things to Think About

- The spirit of camaraderie is quite evident in the way we interact with others on pilgrimage. How can you become a better companion on this journey called life?
- In her poem, Christina Rossetti asks the question, "Does the road wind up-hill all the way?" and answers in the affirmative, "Yes, to the very end." How do you keep hope alive on the up-hill climb?

Good and upright is the LORD;
  therefore he instructs sinners in the way.
He leads the humble in what is right,
  and teaches the humble his way.
All the paths of the LORD are steadfast love and faithfulness,
  for those who keep his covenant and his decrees.
                                              (Psalm 25:8-10)

❧ Day 37: Inner Work

The next time I go on pilgrimage, I'll be ready to do deep inner work. I'll also know that some will not be able to do this and will need to be carried along gently by the rest of the community. Others will never get there. It is not within them. It is my task to live with humbleness of heart among them.

This inner work involves taking on Christ's habits and actions. This can't be brought about solely by my efforts. The transformation of my desires and emotions is brought about only by the renewing and cleansing power of the Spirit. That is why I knelt at ancient altars for many hours throughout the trip. I wanted to assist the Holy Spirit in this change within me, the one who needed it the most. And in my self-examination, I sought to uncover within myself the disordered emotions and desires that most needed cleansing and redirecting. Disappointment and pain, covetousness and clinging, depression and anger—all seedbeds of sin—needed to be opened and healed by God's Spirit. "Come, Holy Spirit, Come."

Pilgrimage is not all about me and mine. It is not about what is best for the individual, but what is best for the community as the Body of Christ. It means taking the time to do the deep, Spirit-led inner work. It is knowing that I am doing the best that I can for who I am and for what I know in the moment—as inadequate and sinful as that is—and trusting that others are doing the same. This ongoing forgiveness toward one another is a basic necessity.

Carlo Carretto, who lived desert spirituality, wrote about this willingness to live in ways that allow others to see our inadequacies and sinfulness: "This road leads to the way of the cross and the crucifixion of the ego. You will be buried with Christ, which is a prelude to being resurrected with him forever."[33]

Moments of Devotion

May I be ready to do deep inner work even as I live with humbleness of heart with others.

Some Things to Think About

- In a self-examination, how are you learning to live with humbleness of heart?
- In the midst of disappointment and pain, covetousness and clinging, depression and anger, are you able to say, "Come, Holy Spirit, come," in order to be healed?

Walk about Zion, go all around it,
  count its towers,
consider well its ramparts;
  go through its citadels,
that you may tell the next generation
  that this is God,
our God forever and ever.
  He will be our guide forever. (Psalm 48:12-14)

❧ Day 38: Expect the Holy Spirit

The next time I'm on pilgrimage, I'll be more open to the unexpectedness of the Holy Spirit, who gives new eyes to see and new ears to hear. Plans change. I'll attend more deeply to the Spirit.

We must work with the Holy Spirit, who convinces us of our truth and reality—a rebirth of our heart and soul and mind. There are a variety of ways that the Holy Spirit breaks hearts open. As you allow the Holy Spirit to work, you will find the destination that your soul has been longing for. Remember, a destination is not an end but the opening to a whole new experience.

Pilgrimage is both the journey and the destination. The two are intertwined. As a pilgrim, I set out for a destination, for a purpose. The journey refined the purpose and gave it new significance each day.

On the final evening of our pilgrimage, we stayed with the Benedictine sisters of Mont Marie. After a splendid dinner, I remained at table to talk with a man who was also lodging there. He was traveling alone and recording his adventures through pen and ink drawings. They were wonderful.

When he left the dining hall, I sat alone, thankful for the stillness. Then I began to carefully place one dish upon another and carry them into the pantry. It felt refreshing to do the ordinary. One of the sisters appeared, and we worked together in silence. She educated me on how to use the brush and pan to sweep the crumbs from the tables and how to remove the wine spots with a spray and cloth. I matched her movements of flowing grace until the last dish was replaced in its cupboard. When all was finished, we wordlessly bowed to each other in gratitude. I extended a smile first to her and then to myself as we climbed the stairs to the chapel for evening prayer. God was looking out for me and gracing me with all the companionship I needed for this final leg of my journey.

Basil Hume, a twentieth-century spiritual leader of the English and Welsh, reflected, "The way is often rough for a pilgrim and hard going, but pilgrims must keep going resolutely and courageously. They are lost if they stop looking for the right way to reach their destination. But there is one who is on the look-out to guide us; it is the Son of God who is the way, the truth and the life."[34]

Moments of Devotion

May I attend more deeply to the Spirit who convinces me of my truth and reality—a rebirth of my heart, soul, and mind.

Some Things to Think About

- Knowing that the Holy Spirit breaks hearts open, are you ready to find the destination that your soul has been longing for? In what ways?
- A destination is not an end but the opening to a whole new experience. When have you reached a destination to discover another open door?

When the LORD restored the fortunes of Zion,
we were like those who dream.
Then our mouth was filled with laughter,
and our tongue with shouts of joy;
then it was said among the nations,
"The LORD has done great things for them."
The LORD has done great things for us,
and we rejoiced.
Restore our fortunes, O LORD,
like the watercourses in the Negeb.
May those who sow in tears
reap with shouts of joy.
Those who go out weeping,
bearing the seed for sowing,
shall come home with shouts of joy,
carrying their sheaves. (Psalm 126)

🕊 Day 39: Leaving the Past

The next time I'm on pilgrimage, I'll be ready for a new life when I return home—whether home be a literal place or a place in my heart. I know that I may not leave my past behind, but I will be changed. This poem and prayer by the great spiritual teacher Thomas Merton seems to express it well for all of us:

> My Lord God, I have no idea where I am going. I do not see the road ahead of me. I cannot know for certain where it will end. Nor do I really know myself, And that fact that I think I am following your will does not mean that I am actually doing so. But I believe that my desire to please you does in fact please you. And I hope I have that desire in all that I am doing. I hope that I will never do anything apart from that desire. And I know that if I do this you will lead me by the right road, though I may know nothing about it. Therefore I will trust you always though I may seem to be lost and in the shadow of death. I will not fear, for you are ever with me, and you will never leave me to face my perils alone.[35]

Moments of Devotion

May I be ready for my new life as I return "home," to face the shadows and perils and to fear not.

Some Things to Think About

- What primary spiritual experiences and God-moments from your past have merged to make you who you are today?
- Perhaps the ultimate trust is evident in that moment when we lie in the shadow of death. Do you have that kind of absolute trust in God?

I will extol you, O LORD, for you have drawn me up,
and did not let my foes rejoice over me.
O LORD my God, I cried to you for help,
and you have healed me.
O LORD, you brought up my soul from Sheol,
restored me to life from among those gone down to the Pit.
Sing praises to the LORD, O you his faithful ones,
and give thanks to his holy name.
For his anger is but for a moment;
his favor is for a lifetime.
Weeping may linger for the night,
but joy comes with the morning. (Psalm 30:1-5)

❧ Day 40: At Pilgrimage End

Today my pilgrimage ends. I have made the toilsome journey through the repentance of Lent and on into the alleluias of Easter to the fire of Pentecost with so many saints who have walked before me. "Therefore, since we are surrounded by so great a cloud of witnesses, let us also lay aside every weight and the sin that clings so closely, and let us run with perseverance the race that is set before us" (Hebrews 12:1). I have been humbled once again by the walk of discipleship. "Humility saith, I am nothing, I have nothing. Love saith, I covet nothing, but one, and that is Jesus."[36]

As I walked in the footsteps of Jesus, as did the saints of old and those of the community of the faithful, I became one with all who had gone before. As John Bunyan wrote in *The Pilgrim's Progress*, "There also you shall meet with thousands and ten thousands that have gone before us to that place; none of them are hurtful, but loving and holy; every one walking in the sight of God, and standing in his presence with acceptance forever. In a word, there we shall see the elders with their golden crowns."[37]

While in France, the past suddenly became present. Now as I sit at home, there is an immediate awareness of the Holy. I sense the Holy when I think of the miraculous that took place at a certain basilica or in the presence of a certain relic. With the community of the saints, I take my rightful place in the cloud of witnesses and add my testimony to these places of prayer.

Origen, a third-century theologian, wrote,

> Understand, then, if you can, what the pilgrimages of the soul are in which it laments with groaning and grief that it has been on pilgrimage so long. We understand these pilgrimages only dully and darkly so long as the pilgrimage still lasts. But then the soul has returned to its rest, that is, to the fatherland in paradise, it will be taught more truly and will understand more truly what the meaning of its pilgrimage was.[38]

As I type these final reflections, I wonder how deeply I believe that the truer lessons are yet to come.

Moments of Devotion

May I view life as a pilgrimage and remember that the journey is life itself.

Some Things to Think About

- Someday we, too, will take our rightful places with the cloud of witnesses. With what member of the "community of the saints" do you look forward to being reunited?
- Can you truly pray, "Humility saith, I am nothing, I have nothing. Love saith, I covet nothing, but one, and that is Jesus"? How are you living that reality?

Notes

Introduction

1. Origen, *Contra Celsus*, Book 1, chapter 51, http://www.earlychristian writings.com/text/origen161.html.

Day 1

2. *Sancti Columbani Opera*, ed. G. S. M. Walker (Dublin, 1970), 97, quoted in Philip Sheldrake, *Living Between Worlds: Place and Journey in Celtic Spirituality* (Cambridge, Mass.: Cowley Publications, 1995), 61.

Day 2

3. Francis Bourdeau, "Pilgrimage, Eucharist, Reconciliation," *Lumen Vitae* 39 (1984): 401.

Day 4

4. The Cavalier Santo Brasca, quoted in John Davies, *Pilgrimage Yesterday and Today* (New York, London: SCM Press, 2000), 42.

5. Jonathan Sumption, *Pilgrimage—An Image of Mediaeval Religion* (Totowa, N.J.: Rowman and Littlefield, 1975), 168.

Day 7

6. Ibid., 121.

7. Helen Bacovcin, trans., *The Way of a Pilgrim* (New York: Doubleday, 1992), 9.

Day 9

8. Douglas C. Vest, *On Pilgrimage* (Boston: Cowley Publications 1998), 128.

Day 10

9. Philip Sheldrake, *Spirituality and History* (Maryknoll, N.Y.: Orbis Books, 1991), 117-18.

10. Brother John of Taizé, "The Pilgrimage Seen through the Bible," *Lumen Vitae* 39 (1984): 381.

Notes

Day 11
11. Bacovcin, 123.

12. Brother Ramon, *The Heart of Prayer: Finding a time, a place and a way to pray* (San Francisco: HarperSanFrancisco, 1995), 121.

Day 12
13. Hans von Campenausen, *Celtic Christian Spirituality* (New York: Continuum International Publishers, 1999), 38.

14. "Pilgrimages," *New Catholic Encyclopedia* (Farmington Hills, Mich.: Gale Group, 1967), 187.

15. C. Leeu, *Tboeck van den Leven Ons Liefs Heeren Jhesu Christi* (The Book of the Life of Our Dear Lord Jesus Christ) (1488), cited in Reindert L. Falkenburg, *Joachim Patinir: Landscape as an Image of the Pilgrimage of Life* (Amsterdam/Philadelphia: John Benjamins, 1988), 98.

Day 13
16. Sir Walter Raleigh, "The Pilgrimage," *The Fireside Encyclopædia of Poetry*, ed. Henry T. Coates (Philadelphia: Henry T. Coates & Co., 1901), 598.

Day 16
17. Alan Jones, *Passion for Pilgrimage* (San Francisco: HarperSanFrancisco, 1989), 12.

Day 18
18. Columba Stewart, *Prayer and Community: The Benedictine Tradition* (Maryknoll, N.Y.: Orbis Books, 1998), 22.

Day 20
19. Anne Dumoulin, "Towards a Psychological Understanding of the Pilgrim," *Lumen Vitae* 32 (1977): 109.

Day 21
20. Kosuke Koyama, *Pilgrim or Tourist: 50 Short Meditations* (London: Christian Journals Ltd., 1975), 1-3.

Day 22
21. Peace Pilgrim, *Peace Pilgrim: Her Life and Work in Her Own Words* (Santa Fe: Ocean Tree, 1994), 25.

22. Ibid., vi.

23. Ronald Finucane, *Miracles and Pilgrims: Popular Beliefs of Medieval England* (New York: Saint Martin's Press, 1995), 85.

24. Ibid., 46.

Day 23

25. John Skinner, *The Book of Margery Kempe* (New York: Doubleday, 1998), 46.

Day 24

26. C. Jones, G. Wainright, and E. Yarnold, eds., *The Study of Spirituality* (New York: Oxford University Press, 1986), 566.

Day 25

27. Søren Kierkegaard and Arthur Dahl, *Soren Kierkegaard's Pilgrimage to Jutland*, trans. T. H. Croxall (Palo Alto, Calif.: Stanford University Press, 1958), 29-30.

28. Mother Columba Hart, trans., *Hadewijch: The Complete Works* (Mahwah, N.J.: Paulist Press, 1980), 78-79.

Day 28

29. Thomas Merton, *The Asian Journal of Thomas Merton* (New York: New Directions, 1973), 5.

Day 29

30. Joan D. Chittister, *A Passion for Life: Fragments of the Face of God* (Maryknoll, N.Y.: Orbis Books, 1996), 43-46.

Day 32

31. Christopher Lewis, "On Going to Sacred Places," *Theology* (September 1989): 393.

Day 36

32. Christina Rossetti, "Up-Hill" (1861), in *Goblin Market, The Price's Progress and Other Poems*, 3rd Edition (Mineola, N.Y.: Dover Publications, 1994), 194.

Day 37
33. Carlo Carretto and Alison Swaisland Bucci, *The Desert Journal: A Diary* (Maryknoll, N.Y.: Orbis Books, 1992), 82-83.

Day 38
34. Basil Hume, *To Be a Pilgrim* (Winnipeg, Manitoba: St. Paul Publications, 1988), 39.

Day 39
35. Thomas Merton, *Thoughts in Solitude* (New York: Farrar, Straus & Cudahy, 1958), 83.

Day 40
36. Walter Hilton, *The Scale of Perfection*, Classics of Western Spirituality (New York: Paulist Press, 1991), 188.

37. John Bunyan, *The Pilgrim's Progress* (Pittsburgh: Whitaker House, 1981), 93.

38. *Origen: Selected Writings*, Classics of Western Spirituality, trans. Rowan A. Greer (New York/Mahwah, N.J.: Paulist Press, 1979), 250.

Other Resources to Continue Your Journey

Collis, Louise. *Memoirs of a Medieval Woman: The Life and Times of Margery Kempe*. New York: Harper & Row, 1983.

Born in Norfolk in 1373, Kempe wrote a single manuscript—her autobiography, which was discovered only in the twentieth century. Read her description of her pilgrimage to Compostela during the Middle Ages.

Lash, Jennifer. *On Pilgrimage: A Time to Seek*. New York: Bloomsbury Publishing, 1999.

Travel with this modern-day pilgrim to Lourdes, Lisieux, and Taizé as well as the numerous stops of the Vézelay pilgrimage—and, of course, Santiago de Compostela.

York, Sarah. *Pilgrim Heart: The Inner Journey Home*. San Francisco: Jossey-Bass, 2001.

The cover alone sells the book, and you won't be disappointed as York offers her firsthand account of her soul-journey. Going on a pilgrimage demands a willingness to face the unfamiliar and unexpected in order to change and grow.

.